UNCLE JOHN'S
Under
the
Slimy Sea

BATHROOM READER®
FOR KIDS ONLY

by the
Bathroom Readers'
Institute

Bathroom Readers' Press
Ashland, Oregon

*UNCLE JOHN'S
UNDER THE SLIMY SEA
BATHROOM READER®
FOR KIDS ONLY*

For information, write:
Bathroom Readers' Institute
P.O. Box 1117, Ashland, OR 97520
www.bathroomreader.com

Cover design by Dale Champlin

Illustrations by Scott G. Brooks
www.scottgbrooks.com

*Uncle John's Under the Slimy Sea
Bathroom Reader For Kids Only*
by the Bathroom Readers' Institute

ISBN-10: 1-59223-711-8
ISBN-13: 978-1592-23711-1
Library of Congress Control Number: 2007928255

Printed in the United States of America
First printing 2007
07 08 09 10 11 5 4 3 2 1

READERS' RAVES

From some of our favorite readers!

"OK, I'll start by saying that *Uncle John's Bathroom Readers* are probably the greatest idea since PB & J! My entire family reads your books. We share, we trade, then we have little sit-downs about the funniest article of the day."

—**Brad**

"I just wanted to say how much I enjoy reading your books. They are really fun to read. I learn so much from them. Thank you."

—**Kathleen**

"I am a 12 year old 6th grader, and I read my *Bathroom Readers* everywhere in the house at all times of day. I LOVE them!!!"

—**Jake**

"Your books are tremendous!!!! Stupendous!!!!! They're absolutely outstanding!!!!"

—**Angela**

"I am 13 and I love your books!!!! I can never go to the bathroom without my mom yelling at me because I take soooo long reading my *Bathroom Readers*!"

—**Michael**

TABLE OF CONTENTS

TWO GIANT SEA FACTS

• The giant squid has the largest eyes of any creature. They're the size of soccer balls.

• The sperm whale's brain can weigh more than 15 pounds, making it the largest brain of any animal's on Earth

INTRODUCTION
Notes from an old Sea Dog

Ahoy, Kids!
It's me, Porter the Wonder Dog. As a Portuguese Water Dog (that's really what I am), I thought I knew a thing or two about the sea. But it turns out there's more to it than just "it's wet, and you swim in it." Other things swim in it, too. There's sharks, lobsters, sharks, krill, sharks, whales, sharks, plankton, sharks, dolphins, and a whole lot of other slimy, finny, and scary creatures. And sharks.

The sea is full of humans, too—from fierce pirates and undersea explorers to surfers, divers, and shipwreck survivors. And that's not all. *Under the Slimy Sea* takes you to the lost city of Atlantis, and introduces you to mermaids and mythological monsters.

But wait! There's more! We have fish that bite (not just sharks), fish that fight, fish that change color, fish that walk, and fish that fly. And let's not forget the slimy parts: hagfish, globsters (eewww!), a forest of seaweed, and SNOT BALLS (double eewww!). So snorkel up, pull on your fins, and dive into the slimy sea!

And, like the sailors say,

Go with the Flow!

THANK YOU

The Bathroom Readers' Institute thanks those people whose help has made this book possible.

Gordon Javna

Jahnna Beecham

Malcolm Hillgartner

Amy Miller

Scott Brooks

Maggie McLaughlin

Dale Champlin

Jay Newman

Brine Boone

Julia Papps

Thom Little

Jeff Altemus

John Dollison

Judy Hadlock

Lisa Meyers

Sydney Stanley

JoAnn Padgett

Caitlin and McKenzie

Dash and Skye

Scarab Media

Steven Style Group

Melinda Allman

Laurel, Mana, and Dylan

Shobha Grace

Porter the Wonder Dog

Thomas Crapper

Mrs. Paul

Charlie the Tuna

the Sturgeon General

Carpo Marx

Marlin Brando

Gillary Duff

Prawn Connery

...and the nation of Finland

MR. BLOBBY

People have always wondered what lurks in the deepest parts of the ocean. Now scientists are beginning to find out—and the results aren't pretty...

Meet Mr. Blobby. He's a *blobfish*. (He's sometimes called a *fathead fish*, too, but why add insult to injury?) He's only one foot in length, and lives 3,000 feet below the surface. This part of the ocean is called the *mesopelagic* zone, also known as the "twilight zone" because very little sunlight reaches it. This guy looks like a blob of Jell-O because that's pretty much what he is. His goopy flesh is just a bit lighter than water, so he doesn't need to use any muscles or oxygen to keep from sinking to the bottom. Like many creatures that live at this great depth, blobfish are "sit-and-wait" predators—they wait patiently for their dinner to drift within reach of their mouths. Then...*gulp!*

DOLPHIN FACTS

➤ Dolphins are born with mustaches. (So are whales.)

➤ A dolphin can hold its breath for up to eight minutes and dive as deep as 1,000 feet.

➤ Dolphins never take a drink. They absorb all their water from their food.

➤ Dolphins sleep with one eye shut—half of their brain rests; the other half (and the other eye) stays awake.

➤ Every dolphin has signature whistles, or "names," that it uses to find its family and friends.

The largest dolphin is the *orca*, or killer whale, which can grow to 31.5 feet long (about 10 meters).

➤ The smallest? It's a tie between Hector's dolphin and the black dolphin. Adults can be as short as four feet long (1.2 meters).

OCEAN ACROBATS

Dolphins are graceful and athletic. They're the stars of aquarium shows the world over, dazzling audiences with soaring flips and dives. But the superstars are the *spinner dolphins*. These mammals got their name from their signature jump: They can leap out of the water and rotate up to seven times, like an ice skater doing an axel jump. Spinners have other great moves, too: tail slaps, fluke dives, nose-outs, and spectacular head-over-tail flips.

Like all dolphins, spinners love to play. One of their favorite games is "make a play-toy." Anything floating in the water—a fishing float, a lump of driftwood—becomes "it." Spinners will play catch with the object, and even wear it on their heads like a hat. They're so much fun to watch that Hawaiians call them "Ambassadors of Aloha."

Dolphin researchers have studied spinners to figure out why they jump and spin, and have come up with a few explanations. Sometimes they spin to get rid of a pesky parasite. Sometimes a spinner wants to signal the rest of the pod exactly where it is (in this case, the spin ends with a loud belly-flop). But the best explanation for why spinners spin is, well, because they can.

IS SAND FISH POOP?

Well, some of it is—particularly on the coral reefs of the Indian and Pacific Oceans. Coral are actually small animals, related to sea anemones, that protect their soft bodies with a limestone covering. Coral gather in colonies that number in the millions. Each new generation of coral builds on the skeleton of the previous one, and over time coral reefs become home to all kinds of sea life. Those limestone skeletons are literally hard as a rock, but that doesn't bother the *bumphead parrotfish*.

Bumpheads love to eat the algae that grow on the coral. Rather than pick it off bit by bit, they use their strong jaws to chomp right through the rock, which they swallow along with the algae. Then they poop it out as fine white sand. On a single reef, bumpheads can crank out a ton of sand every year. Over centuries the sand builds up to make tropical islands. So those beautiful white beaches you see on postcards of tropical paradises are really nothing but a load of fish poop!

GNARLY TEETH

QUESTION:

What's got a hard shell, weighs more than 1,000 pounds, and has a mouthful of truly gnarly "teeth"?

ANSWER:
THE LEATHERBACK TURTLE

Well, maybe not *actually* teeth. What this ocean reptile has is a mouthful of stiff spines that point backwards to help it swallow its favorite food—jellyfish!

MONSTER WAVES

So you want to be a sailor? You may change your mind after you read this.

WALL OF WATER

What's a monster wave? One that rises 80 feet or more above the ocean's surface. Imagine a wall of water ¼ mile wide and as high as a 10-story building bearing down on

you like a freight train. That's a monster wave! Sometimes they're called "freaks" and "rogues." The biggest wave ever measured at sea was 98 feet tall. Most monster waves are caused by hurricanes and other storms. Others happen when waves join great ocean currents like the Gulf Stream. But wherever they come from, they're deadly— monster waves can snap a giant tanker ship in half like a toothpick. Worst of all, it takes hundreds of miles for one to build up to monster size. A ship can be sailing on a clear day far from a storm and still get slammed by a monster wave.

HOOK, LINE, AND SINKER

Q: *What do you call a fish with no eye?*
A: FSH!

Q: *How do you keep a fish from smelling?*
A: Cut off its nose.

Q: *If fish lived on land, which country would they live in?*
A: Finland.

Q: *What did the boy octopus say to the girl octopus?*
A: I want to hold your hand hand hand hand hand hand hand hand.

Q: *Why are fish smarter than mice?*
A: Because they live in schools.

SEA ANIMAL QUIZ #1: WHAT IS THIS MYSTERIOUS GIANT?

IT'S BIG...

...As in the biggest creature that ever lived. In fact, this giant is larger than a brontosaurus and a Tyrannosaurus rex put together.

- Its tongue weighs as much as an elephant.
- Its heart is as big as a car.
- Some of its blood vessels are so wide that a person could swim down them.

REALLY BIG...

The largest one ever measured was 108 feet long and weighed almost 190 *tons*. If you stood one on its tail, it would be as tall as a 10-story building. You'd have to stack up more than 25 elephants to equal its weight.

AND FAST...

It can swim at speeds of up to 48 mph, making it one of the fastest swimmers in the world.

AND HUNGRY...

It spends its summers in the icy waters around Antarctica eating *krill*, tiny shrimp-like crustaceans that live there in huge swarms. A single one of these creatures can eat 40 million krill in a day.

AND LOUD!

Our mystery mammal is the loudest creature ever recorded. A jet plane can reach a volume of 120 decibels. A gunshot might hit 140 decibels. But this monster's call clocks in at 180 decibels and can be heard for thousands of miles underwater.

WHAT IS IT?

ANSWER:

THE BLUE WHALE!

This marvelous creature is also one of the most mysterious. Scientists are just beginning to understand some of its habits, but there's much they still don't know, such as where it breeds, or where it migrates. Sadly, we may never find out because the blue whale has been hunted almost to extinction. Almost half a million were killed in the 19th century for their blubber. Scientists guess that there might be as few as 2,000 left. Because they are so rare, today there is a worldwide ban on hunting the blue whale.

FIERCE GUARDIANS

Swimming in Hawaii? Don't forget your aumakua!

Many Hawaiians believe that guardian spirits protect their family. The guardians, known as *aumakua*, often take the form of a powerful animal, such as the shark. As long as the family takes care of their *aumakua*, the shark will take care of them.

• In the 1930s, a tour boat sank off the island of Molokai. Sharks attacked and everyone was killed…except the captain, who later said he had called his *aumakua*. When the shark appeared, it offered the captain its dorsal fin and pulled the man safely past the other sharks to the shore.

• A man from Maui and his wife were sailing to a neighboring island when a sudden squall capsized the boat and swept them into the rough seas. As they foundered in the water, the man called out, "If I have any *aumakua* in this ocean, I pray you to carry us to the land." A streak flashed by them and a shark appeared in the water. They grabbed the shark by the tail, and it towed them safely to shore.

THE BERMUDA TRIANGLE

*Planes and boats check
in, but they don't
check out.*

In 1918 a ship called the *U.S.S. Cyclops* sailed into an area of water off the Florida coast…and vanished. There were 309 people aboard and not one person, nor a lifeboat or even a scrap of wood, was ever found. For hundreds of years, people have been talking about this

expanse of ocean that stretches from Bermuda to Florida to Puerto Rico, known as the Bermuda Triangle. Records show that more than 1,000 people have vanished there— which may be the reason some people also call it the Devil's Triangle.

Even as far back as 1492, Christopher Columbus reported trouble on his first voyage to the New World when he crossed the Bermuda Triangle. He and his crew observed strange lights hovering over the ocean, and noted in the ship's log that their compass suddenly went haywire.

MAYDAY! MAYDAY!

In 1945 five U.S. Navy Avenger torpedo bombers flew over that area during a military training exercise. Two hours into the mission, the pilots sent this radio message: "Everything is wrong. The ocean doesn't look as it should." All five planes in the squadron reported that their compasses were spinning and they couldn't tell north from south. They said the sky was a strange yellow color…and then they were gone. The Navy immediately sent another plane with a crew of 13 men to help. That plane disappeared, too.

Where did they go? The Navy searched for weeks, but not a single clue was found. The planes had simply vanished. More than 100 ships and planes have disappeared into the Triangle. Ships have been found drifting in the area with all of the passengers missing. Sometimes a dog or a bird will be left behind, but never a human. Pilots flying over the area will be having a normal radio conversation with ground control and suddenly they're gone, as if they've flown into a hole in the sky.

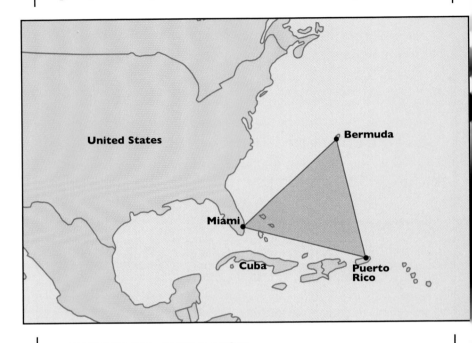

UNSOLVED MYSTERY

What causes compasses to go wild and lights to appear in the sky? Some say that in this area of the ocean is a pocket of magnetic energy that affects electronic gear. Others speak of black holes that send planes and ships into some kind of time warp. Geologist Dr. Richard McIver thought that undersea landslides might cause the release of huge amounts of methane gas which would make the sea look like it's boiling and create clouds of odd-colored light. Some folks whisper about aliens in UFOs abducting the people and planes.

What do *you* think?

FALSE ALARM

Ew. What's that smell?

In December 2006, an alarm went off in the aquarium at the Weymouth Sea Life Center in England. Marine biologist Sarah Leaney raced to the tank to see what was wrong, but found nothing out of order. As she looked at the alarm sensor, a sea turtle floating by ripped off a couple of farts that set the alarm off again. Leaney quickly realized what had happened: The staff had fed the turtle a holiday treat of Brussels sprouts. It seemed that vegetable has the same effect of turtles as it does on people when they eat too much of it—it produces a mighty, stinky wind!

THE WORLD'S SAFEST BEACH? HA!

New Smyrna Beach, Florida, may be the shark bite capital of the world.

According to the International Shark Attack File, two-thirds of all shark attacks in the United States occur in Volusia County, Florida. Most of those take place at New Smyrna Beach, a place once advertised by local businessmen as "the world's safest bathing beach." In August 2001, ten people, most of them surfers, were bitten in as many days. The "world's safest beach" was closed for 10 days while thousands of black-tip sharks cruised by off the coast on their annual migration north. Experts used to think black-tip sharks weren't a threat to people...but not any more!

PREY
(aka "doofuses, sharkbait")

PREDATORS
(they're everywhere!)

SHARK FACTS

➤ Sharks have no bones. Their skeletons are made of cartilage, the same stuff that's in your ears and your nose.

➤ Sharks are ancient. They were patrolling the oceans more than 300 million years ago—nearly 75 million years before the dinosaurs were around.

➤ Scientists think sharks were the first creatures to have teeth.

➤ A shark can detect a single drop of blood in a million drops (25 gallons) of water.

➤ If it doesn't swim, a shark will sink.

➤ Sharks can sense vibrations in water, and they can detect electrical currents. They use these skills to find their prey.

FISH SALON

If cleaner fish could speak, their
favorite word would be, "Next!"

L ife for a fish is tough. It spends every waking minute trying to eat other fish and avoid being eaten. But there's one class of fish that gets a free pass from the "I'm gonna eat you first" rule: cleaner fish. These tiny fish (mostly *wrasses* and *gobies* the size of minnows) have carved out a special niche for themselves in the sea.

Most fish suffer from parasites—little bugs that latch onto scales and gills like ticks on a dog. But unlike dogs, fish can't scratch. So they line up at cleaning stations set up by cleaner fish in caves or overhangs. The cleaner fish crowd around each "customer" fish and nibble off all of the pests. They even do a teeth cleaning, swimming safely in and out of the gaping jaws of their guests. They work hard, too—researchers on Australia's Great Barrier Reef logged some cleaner fish servicing 2,000 fish a day.

Being a cleaner isn't just a job for fish. There are cleaner shrimp, and even seagulls. But it's a sweet deal for the ones that take on the job: They get an unlimited supply of food (up to 1,200 parasites a day—yum!), and best of all, they don't get eaten by their clients.

DID YOU KNOW...

...the world's only underwater mailbox can be found 32.8 feet below the surface in Susami Bay, Japan? Diver Heinze Pieorkowski put it there on April 23, 1999, but he didn't say why.

FLIPPER

The first dolphin superstar was a female named Mitzi.

One night a stuntman named Ricou Browning was watching the TV show *Lassie* with his kids and thought, "Wouldn't it be great to do a show like this with a boy and a dolphin?" Ricou took his idea to producer Ivan Tors, and the movie *Flipper* was born. A dolphin

named Mitzi was chosen to be the star. Mitzi was smart: She could fetch five things at once, tow a boat with a rope, shake hands, hit the water with her tail, and give someone a ride with her flipper. Her best trick was carrying a boy on her back, which she learned by playing fetch: One day Ricou tossed his nine-year-old son into the water and told Mitzi to retrieve him. The dolphin put her fin under the boy's arm and brought him right back.

The movie *Flipper* came out in 1963, and was a huge success. Another movie was made, followed by a TV series. By then Mitzi had retired. She was replaced by another female dolphin named Suzy, who played Flipper from 1964 to 1967.

SEA DOGS

Aye, matey, it's those two-legged scourges of the sea—pirates.

BLACKBEARD. The most feared pirate of them all was Blackbeard, a true Pirate of the Caribbean. Blackbeard (his real name was Edward Teach) went into battle with six pistols strapped across his chest and smoking fuses woven into his wild hair and beard. This merciless villain was known to shoot his own crew because, he said, "If I don't shoot one every now and again, they'll forget who I am." When he discovered that the woman he loved had given a ring to another sailor, he attacked her boyfriend's ship and mailed the man's severed hand—with the ring still on it—to the lady. He terrorized the Caribbean and the Atlantic off the Carolina coast from 1716 to 1718 in his ship, *Queen Anne's Revenge*. His final battle was against the *Pearl*, a British ship led by pirate hunter Robert Maynard. Trapped in a shallow bay, Blackbeard fought like a madman to the end. Maynard wrote in his report that Blackbeard was stabbed 20 times and shot five times before he finally fell. They cut off the pirate's head and hung it from the

bowsprit as a warning to all other pirate wannabes. But Blackbeard had the last word. Legend has it that when his headless body was thrown overboard, it swam around the *Pearl* five times...looking for its head.

BARTHOLOMEW ROBERTS. "Black Bart"
Roberts came to piracy late (he was 37), but he was the most successful pirate of all time. Born in Wales, he roamed the seas from Brazil to Africa to Newfoundland, capturing and looting more than 400 ships during his career. He designed his own pirate flag, which had a giant figure of himself, cutlass in hand, standing on two skulls. Roberts' life of crime came to an end when he was killed by a hail of gunfire in a battle off the coast of West Africa in 1722.

BLACK CAESAR. Henri "Black" Caesar was born
a slave in Haiti in 1765. He worked in a sawmill, where he was mistreated by a white overseer. In 1791 Haitian slaves revolted against their masters and Caesar joined the fight, starting first by executing his overseer with a crosscut saw. When peace came in 1804, he turned to piracy and quickly became feared across the Caribbean for his ferocity in battle and his skill as a sailor. He later moved his base to the west coast of Florida, and is supposed to have buried millions in loot on Sanibel Island. Unlike most pirates of his day, Black Caesar didn't end his life at the end of a rope. In fact, no one knows what became of him. He just vanished.

MADAME CHING

One of the greatest pirates of all time was...a woman!

Madame Ching terrorized the waters off the coast of China in the early years of the 19th century. At the height of her power, she commanded a fleet of 1,800 ships and 70,000 men. But she didn't get to the top by being nice. If one of her pirates broke her rules, she had his head lopped off.

Although Madame Ching terrorized the Chinese navy for years, she was able to do what few pirates ever accomplished: die of old age. In exchange for giving up piracy, the Chinese Navy granted her a pardon in 1810. Madame Ching was even allowed to keep all of her stolen treasure. She used it to open up a gambling house, which she ran for the rest of her life.

YO HO HO!

Avast, ye landlubbers! If ye wanna be a pirate, get your sea legs and take this quiz afore ye set sail.

1. When a pirate is *tipping the blackspot,* he is:

a) Making a death threat.

b) Swabbing a dirty deck.

c) Removing his eye patch.

d) Asking for the pepper.

2. What is a *poop deck?*

a) The place where seagulls like to poop on a ship.

b) The deck above the captain's quarters at the stern (rear) of the ship.

c) Where pirates go to the bathroom, also known as the "head."

d) A deck of cards with all the aces missing.

3. When a pirate says "shiver me timbers," he's saying:

a) It's cold out here, matey!

b) The wind's a-blowing and the ship's a creaking.

c) Whoa…what the heck was that?

d) He's singing a work song. ("Shiver me timbers, hoist them sails; let's get this bucket out of the gale.")

4. What are *long clothes?*

a) Rough weather gear pirates wore when sailing through hurricanes.

b) The dresses female pirates wore.

c) Baggy pants and loose jackets that only landlubbers wore.

d) A type of sail used when running down wind.

5. What is a *Yellow Jack?*

a) Pirate slang for a yellow jacket.

b) The name of a legendary sea monster known to have sunken many a ship to "Davy Jones' locker."

c) A warning flag. When a Yellow Jack is flown, it means there's a contagious illness (like the plague) on board.

d) The name of a famous merman.

6. When a pirate *takes a caulk,* he's:

a) Taking a nap on deck.

b) Brushing his teeth.

c) Going to the bathroom.

d) Shipwrecked on a deserted island.

ANSWERS:

1. a) When a pirate delivers a death threat, he slips his victim a piece of paper with a black smudge on one side.

2. b) A poop deck is the highest deck on a sailing ship.

3. c) He's saying he's as surprised as if his ship had just run aground (which would make the masts shiver).

4. c) Pirates couldn't risk wearing anything loose fitting

5. c) Merchant ships often flew a Yellow Jack to keep pirate ships from attacking them.

6. a) A "caulk" of black tar and rope was stuffed between the planks on a ship's deck to keep water from leaking in. When pirates slept on deck, they'd often wake up with black lines across their faces from the caulk.

STAYIN' ALIVE

This pair shows you how to survive 20,000 feet below the surface.

GROW BIG TEETH

And the sharper, the better. Food is scarce at the bottom

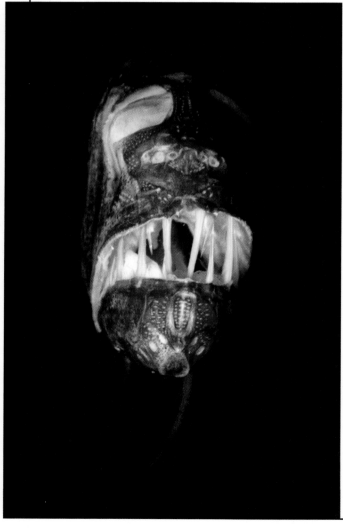

of the ocean. Most creatures survive by eating the scraps that sink down from the surface. Others, like the *sabretooth fish*, will eat anything that passes by—even fish that are bigger than they are.

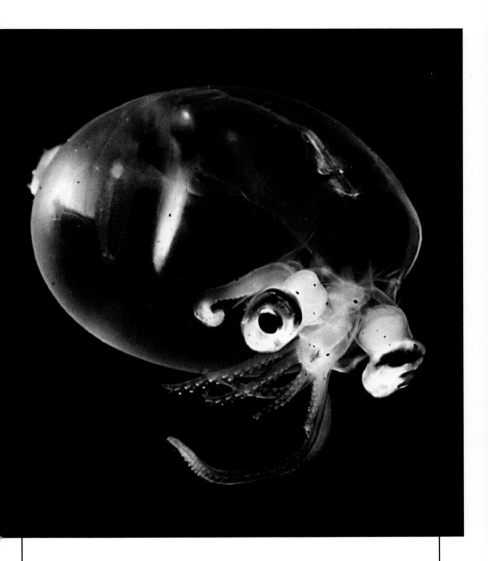

BECOME INVISIBLE

Some creatures living in the dark abyss use skin color (or the lack of color) as camouflage. Many are pitch black and others, like the *deep sea squid*, have no color at all—they are completely transparent. A predator has to bump into one of them to find it.

THE "DEEP" WOODS

Welcome to the kelp forest, where seaweed hundreds of feet high is home to all kinds of sea creatures.

This forest isn't made of trees—it's made of a type of seaweed called *giant kelp*. Kelp forests flourish in cool offshore waters all around the world. Unlike trees, kelp doesn't put down roots in the sand; it latches onto rocks with its finger-like growths called *holdfasts*. And once it does, look out! Kelp can grow 300 feet in a year. That's almost a foot a day! Why does it grow so fast? Because like all plants, kelp need sunlight to live, and the sunlight is up at the surface. As soon as the stipe (stalk) of the kelp plant reaches the ocean surface, its leaves (called *blades*) spread out in a vast canopy, much like the Amazon rain forest, only underwater. That canopy provides a protected shelter for fish, lobsters, crabs, clams, rays, and seals, as well as tons of food for them to eat. Every winter, ocean storms rip many of the kelp plants off the rocks and cast them on shore, destroying the forest. And every spring a new forest grows up to replace the old one.

DOWN, DOWN, WA-A-A-Y DOWN...

How low can you go in the ocean?
Here's a guide to the ocean zones.

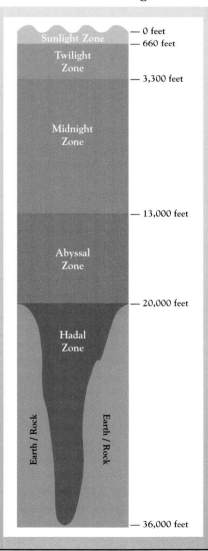

Sunlight Zone	— 0 feet
	— 660 feet
Twilight Zone	
	— 3,300 feet
Midnight Zone	
	— 13,000 feet
Abyssal Zone	
	— 20,000 feet
Hadal Zone	
Earth / Rock Earth / Rock	
	— 36,000 feet

SUNLIGHT ZONE
0–660 feet deep

The *euphotic* zone is the top layer of the ocean, and home to 90% of life in the sea. Why? The sun. Its light and warmth make this a great place for plants to grow, and for the fish and mammals that eat them. But with all that sunlight there's no place to hide, so many species use *countershading* to disguise themselves— they're often dark on top and light on their bellies. From above, they blend with the dark water below; from below, they blend with the bright water above.

THE TWILIGHT ZONE 660–3,300 *feet deep*

Also called the *dysphotic* zone, it's too dim for plants to grow. How do creatures down here survive? By feeding on each other. Inhabitants of this zone have to be able to handle cold temperatures and intense water pressure. Some fish have extra-big eyes to help them see, while others make their own light with special organs in their bodies called *photophores*. Scientists call that process *bioluminescence*. Many twilight zone inhabitants have thin bodies to make it harder for predators to see them. Fish in this zone don't chase their food; they either stalk it...or wait for it.

THE MIDNIGHT ZONE 3,300–13,000 *feet deep*

Also called the *aphotic* zone, this is the first ocean layer where there's no light at all. Here the water is always just above freezing and pitch black. The water pressure can be as great as two tons per square inch! Only 1% of sea life, including the mysterious giant squid, lives in this zone, but some surface animals, such as the sperm whale, can dive down to these depths to hunt them.

THE ABYSSAL ZONE 13,000–20,000 *feet deep*

The *abyssal* zone is the *truly* deep sea, but unlike the desert-like quality of the midnight zone, there's lots of life here. Covering 85% of the ocean floor, this is the single largest habitat on Earth. Most of the deep is a great plain covered in thick goopy mud called *sediment*. The burrowing *sea pig* and other odd creatures of the Deep get their food from eating the muck.

THE HADAL ZONE *20,000–36,000 feet deep*

For most of the ocean, the abyssal zone is as low as you can go. But there are huge canyons in the ocean floor that go far deeper. This is the *Hadal* zone, named for Hades, the ancient Greek god of the Underworld. These great underwater gorges are miles below the surface, and for years scientists believed nothing could survive the crushing water pressure.

Then, in 1960, explorers Jacques Piccard and Don Walsh took a specially built submarine named the *Trieste* to the bottom of the deepest underwater canyon, the Mariana Trench near the Philippines. They dropped to a depth of 35,800 feet—a feat no one has ever matched. To their amazement, they spotted some shrimp-like creatures and flatfish swimming at the bottom of the world.

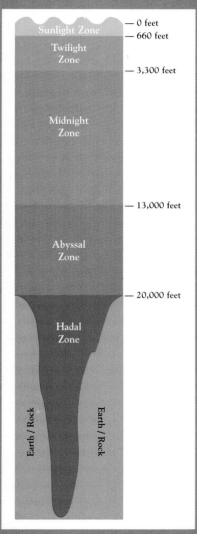

Sunlight Zone — 0 feet
— 660 feet

Twilight Zone

— 3,300 feet

Midnight Zone

— 13,000 feet

Abyssal Zone

— 20,000 feet

Hadal Zone

Earth / Rock　　Earth / Rock

DUMBO

This deep sea octopus swims with its "ears."

"Dumbo" is an octopus that lives 1,000 feet down in the ocean. Until BBC film crews filmed it while making the documentary *The Blue Planet*, no one had ever seen an octopus like it before. Those big flaps behind its eyes look like ears, but they're actually fins. *Grimpoteuthis* (Dumbo's scientific name) swims by pushing water through its funnel, flapping its webbed arms, or paddling with its finny "ears." Or it can use all three methods at the same time. "Dumbo" is less than 5 inches long and likes to swim just above the seafloor, where it can dart down and snag snails and worms. There are actually 14 different types of "Dumbo" octopuses, but other than that we don't know much about them at all.

NO BRAIN?
NO PROBLEM

They don't have brains, hearts, or even bones—
they just drift silently and carry a big sting!

Jellyfish aren't fish. They're invertebrate (boneless) animals related to coral and anemones, and have lived in the seas for over 650 million years. There are more than 2,000 species of them: Some are just an inch wide while others, such as the *Nomura*, have a "bell" (body) larger than a beach umbrella and weigh more than 450 pounds! The monster of all jellyfish is the *Arctic lion's mane*: One was found with a bell more than seven feet wide and tentacles 120 feet long. What the jelly lacks in body parts it makes up for with its sting. Jellyfish have a net of stinging tentacles that paralyze and kill their prey quickly. That keeps a jelly's fragile body from getting torn apart in a struggle.

SPOOK(Y) FISH!

These bug-eyes have a flashlight in their butt!

Discovered by a BBC documentary crew in 1993, *winteria* are known more commonly as *barreleyes* or *spookfish* because of their huge eyes. Spookfish live far below the sunlight zone at depths of up to 6,500 feet, which is why they developed such sensitive eyes. They're tiny, only about six inches long, which is probably why no one found them before. But what's *really* bizarre about this fish is that it has a light organ in its rectum that shines a light out behind it.

Why would a spookfish have the biological equivalent of a flashlight in its butt? Observation revealed that these fish hang vertically in the water, with their big eyes staring up for any prey swimming above them. Scientists think the spookfish probably uses the light shining out of its butt as a form of *counter-illumination* to help it blend in with the dim light coming down from the surface, making the spookfish virtually invisible to its prey.

LOST AT SEA!

"Daddy's a sailor. Why don't we sail around the world?" —Lyn "Mom" Robertson

Neil and Sam Robertson were nine years old when their parents decided to take the family around the world on their boat, a 43-foot schooner called the *Lucette*. Their older brother Douglas and a buddy came along for what promised to be the adventure of a lifetime. It was—only not in the way they imagined.

On June 15, 1972, three orcas attacked the *Lucette* several hundred miles off the Galapagos Islands. Within seconds the orcas had punched two big holes in the bottom of the boat. Then the animals swam off, leaving Neil, Sandy, and the rest of the family with only a few moments to scramble into their life raft. The situation looked hopeless. Their boat had sunk. They were lost in the middle of the Pacific Ocean with no maps, no compass, no radio, and only 18 bottles of water.

EMERGENCY RATIONS

Luckily, their mom had managed to throw a bag of onions, ten oranges, six lemons, and a can of crackers into the raft before the boat sank. Each day Mrs. Robertson fed the family their daily rations: a little piece of onion and a sip of water. Sometimes they had a slice of orange or a bite of the peel. They tried fishing, but sharks broke the lines and took the hooks. Once or twice they were able to catch a sea turtle and eat that.

Drifting in the open boat took a terrible toll on them. Their faces were blistered with sunburn, and their bodies became covered in boils from sitting in saltwater all the time. To make matters worse, sharks circled the raft, waiting for any opportunity to strike. At night Mr. Robertson would beat them away with an oar. To keep up their spirits they told each other stories and sang songs. Somehow it was enough to keep them hanging on.

SHARK TIP

According to experts and survivors, the best thing you can do when a shark attacks is fight back and get out of the water as quickly as possible. Never, ever play dead.

ADRIFT AT SEA

The Robertsons drifted for days, searching the horizon for signs of a passing ship. None came. After a few days, the raft sprang a leak. They pumped air into it, but it continued to take on seawater. So they took turns 24 hours a day scooping water out with a tin cup. Their future looked hopeless.

SAVED!

After 18 days they abandoned the raft and climbed into the nine-foot dinghy they'd taken with them when the *Lucette* went down. That was to be "home" for rest of their ordeal. It finally came to an end when a Japanese fishing boat rescued them. Somehow they had survived on the open ocean for an amazing 38 days!

AND THE WINNER IS...

*Meet some superlative members
of the fish family.*

THE BIGGEST

The largest **whale shark** ever seen was 65 feet long.
That's about 1 ½ times longer than a school bus.

THE SMALLEST

A tiny **carp** from Sumatra is less
than a ⅓ of an inch long. Its
name is *Paedocypris progenitica*.
(Say that 10 times really fast!)

THE FASTEST

The **sailfish** has been
clocked swimming at 67
miles per hour.

THE SLOWEST

The **sea horse** pokes along
at ¹⁄₁₀₀th of a mile per hour.
At that rate, it would
take it six hours to
go the length of a
football field!

THE FIERCEST

There are many candidates for this category, but the **red piranha** from the Amazon River in Brazil probably wins by a fang. Renowned for their feeding frenzies, a school of hungry red piranhas can strip the flesh off a hapless victim in seconds.

THE DEADLIEST

The **box jellyfish**, also called the sea wasp, is the world's deadliest creature. The venom from just one jellyfish can kill 60 people.

THE LONGEST

The **oarfish** is the longest fish in the world. It sports a magnificent red fin that's nearly the same length as its 50-foot snakelike body. That, along with its horselike face and blue gills, accounts for it being the source of many sea serpent sightings.

"ME, QUIT? NEVER!"

It takes more than a shark to keep this kid out of the water.

Bethany Hamilton loves to surf. In fact, this teenager from Hawaii wants to be a professional surfer some day. But an early morning surf session on October 31, 2003, turned into a terrifying fight for her life. Thirteen-year-old Bethany was waiting for a wave on Kauai's north shore when a 14-foot tiger shark attacked her. The shark bit a huge chunk out of the surfboard, along with Bethany's entire left arm. Somehow Bethany managed to paddle back to shore before passing out. By the time friends got her to the hospital, the young surfer had lost nearly 75% of her blood. But she survived…and 10 weeks later, she was out in the water again. At first, she just wanted to see if she could surf with one arm—but once she had that mastered, she started to compete again. And she won! Today Bethany travels around the world, surfing and inspiring others to go for their dreams. As Bethany says in her own words, "Me, quit? Never!"

SHARK BAIT...NOT!

Don't want to become shark bait? Here's what you need to know before you hit the surf.

Of the 375 species of sharks, only 30 are known to attack humans. There are about 70 unprovoked attacks reported worldwide every year. That's a pretty small number when you consider the millions of beachgoers who enter shark territory (shark territory being *any* part of the ocean, *anywhere*). The fact is, you're more likely to be struck by lightning than become a shark snack. But then again, if you've ever been in the ocean, you were probably within 15 feet of a shark and never knew it. So better safe than sorry, right?

1. *Don't go swimming during shark feeding hours—* dawn, dusk, and night.

2. *Swim with friends.* Sharks prefer to attack lone victims.

3. *Don't get in the water if you're bleeding.* Even a small cut is enough to call a shark in from the abyss.

4. *Stay close to shore.* You don't want a shark between you and the beach, and it will be easier for help to reach you if you are attacked.

5. *Don't wear a watch or shiny jewelry* (even earrings) into the water. Your jewelry looks a lot like fish scales to a shark.

6. *Don't wear brightly colored bathing suits—*especially yellow. Shark experts have discovered that sharks are attracted to high contrasts, including uneven tans.

7. If you see a bunch of birds diving into the water, head for the beach. The birds are diving for baitfish, and sharks love baitfish.

8. Don't go swimming where people are fishing— sharks may be fishing there, too.

9. Seeing dolphins around doesn't automatically make you safe. Large sharks hunt dolphins.

10. Don't splash a lot. A shark may mistake you for wounded prey.

11. Stay away from the shark's favorite hunting grounds—steep drop-offs near underwater cliffs or sandbars, polluted water, and murky water.

12. Don't go swimming where sharks have been spotted and never, ever try to touch one. If you see a shark, get out of the water...*fast!*

IT WAS TH-I-I-I-S BIG!

For the record, here are the
biggest creatures ever caught.

• The biggest *blue whale* was captured near the South
Shetland Islands in 1926. It was 108 feet long and
weighed 380,000 pounds.

• A *great white shark* caught off Cuba in 1945 was 21 feet
long and weighed 7,301 pounds.

• A *giant squid* captured in 1878 weighed in at 4,000
pounds, and had tentacles measuring 35 feet in length.

• The biggest *lobster* of all time (nicknamed "Mike")
was caught in 1934. This colossal crustacean weighed a
whopping 42 pounds, 7 ounces.

STINGRAY TO THE RESCUE!

For centuries, people have written tales of sea creatures rescuing sailors lost at sea. But this story happens to be true.

BOY OVERBOARD!

On January 15, 1990, 18-year-old Lottie Stevens and a friend were fishing off the island-nation of Vanuatu in the South Pacific when a fierce storm caught them by surprise. Their boat capsized, drowning Lottie's friend and leaving him clinging to the wreckage of the boat. After three days, the teenager left the floating debris and swam towards what he hoped was land. He swam for two days without getting anywhere. Exhausted, he knew he was finally about to run out of luck. Then he was suddenly lifted out of the water by a stingray! The ray was at least 15 feet long from head to tail.

RAY RIDER

At first, Lottie was terrified—stingrays aren't known to be friendly. But this giant ray carried him on its back night and day for more than two weeks. They passed safely through the shark-infested waters and rough seas until the stingray swam into the shallow waters of New Caledonia, 300 miles from Vanuatu. Lottie was lost at sea for a total of 21 days—16 of them on the back of a stingray.

ALIEN INVASION

They're here! And they're...
jellyfish?

Every autumn the seas off the west coast of Japan are invaded by millions of huge aliens who destroy fishing nets and drive off the salmon and tuna the fishermen usually catch. Although they look like something from another galaxy, these "aliens" aren't from outer space at all. They're a species of jellyfish called *Nomura's jellyfish*—giant jellies over six feet in diameter.

GIANT JELLIES

These seasonal swarms have been happening for years, but for some reason they have recently grown more intense—not just in the Sea of Japan, but around the world. *Purple jellyfish* and *lion's mane jellyfish* invaded European beaches in 2006, and *bluebottle jellies* swarmed the coasts of Australia in January 2007. Scientists think these massive swarms may be a result of global warming and overfishing.

IF YOU CAN'T BEAT 'EM, EAT 'EM!

But the Japanese have come up with a way to fight back:
Local chefs give cooking lessons in how to eat the jellies
(recipes include salted jellyfish with cucumber and soy
sauce). Or you can eat them raw, like sushi. You can
have all the seconds you want, too—at 400 pounds per
Nomura's jellyfish, there are always plenty of leftovers.

MISTER MOM

The most dedicated stay-at-home mom in the sea...is a dad!

Sea horses aren't really horses. They just look like them. These four-inch-long fish swim through the water upright. Their dorsal fins act like boat propellers, sending them forward. When they want to stop, they put on the brakes by grabbing hold of a piece of seaweed or coral with their curly tails.

When sea horses decide to have a family, it's the dad who does the heavy lifting. In fact, sea horses and their cousins, pipefish, are the only species on Earth in which the *dad* gets pregnant. The male sea horse has a pouch just like a kangaroo, into which the mom drops nearly 200 tiny eggs. And for the next month, that's where they grow. When it's time to give birth, the dad becomes a rocking horse: He grabs hold of a seaweed stem and rocks back and forth to launch his baby sea horses into the world.

WATER WORLD

- 71% of the Earth's surface is water.

- 97% of the Earth's water is in the ocean. Less than 1% is fresh water.

- 80% of all life lives in the ocean.

- 99% percent of the living space on the Earth is under water. (Less than 10% of that space has been explored.)

- If you were to stand at the deepest spot in the ocean, the water pressure would feel as if you were trying to lift up fifty Boeing 747s.

- There's enough gold in the ocean to give a nine-pound chunk to every person in the world.

- If you removed the salt in the ocean, you could cover all the land on Earth in a layer of salt five feet deep.

- The weight of the garbage dumped into the ocean every year is more than three times the weight of the fish caught in the same year.

- There's as much ice in Antarctica as there is water in the Atlantic Ocean.

- There are 25,000 islands in the Pacific Ocean—more than all the other islands in the other oceans combined.

- What's the tallest mountain on Earth? It's mostly underwater. Mauna Kea in Hawaii rises 33,465 feet from the ocean floor, beating Mt. Everest by more than 3,000 feet.

MORE SHARK FACTS

➤ Sharks never get cancer. Scientists hope to discover the shark's secret defense to help us create anti-cancer drugs.

➤ The *swell shark* from New Zealand barks like a dog.

➤ Bull sharks are the only sharks that can live in both salt and fresh water. There's a lake in Nicaragua that's full of them.

➤ Here are some of the things that have been found inside a shark's stomach: an alarm clock, an unopened bottle of wine, a drum, a bicycle, a treasure chest, a suit of armor, and a torpedo.

OFF THE DEEP END

Q: *What happened to the fishing boat that sank in piranha-infested waters?*

A: It came back with a skeleton crew.

Q: If they made a movie starring the Loch Ness monster and the great white shark from *Jaws*, what would the movie be called?

A: *Loch Jaws.*

Q: *Why is it so easy to weigh fish?*

A: They have their own scales.

Q: *What sits at the bottom of the sea and shivers?*

A: A nervous wreck.

Q: *What sea animal can be adjusted to play music?*

A: The tune-a fish!

THE BLOOP

*There's something very **loud deep in the ocean.***

DID YOU HEAR THAT?

The ocean is a noisy place. Undersea volcanoes rumble, whales sing, dolphins whistle, and shrimp snap. Scientists have been listening to the sounds for years through a network of underwater microphones. But researchers were startled in 1997 when they heard a noise in the Pacific Ocean, louder than anything they'd ever heard before (the microphones that picked up the sound were over 3,000 miles apart). It sounded like this: "BLOOP."

Was it manmade? No, no one has ever made a machine —not even a bomb—as loud as the Bloop. Was it a whale? No. Blue whales are the loudest animals on the planet, but the Bloop made their call sound like a "peep."

So what was it? Nobody knows.

SURF'S UP—WAY UP!

Ken Bradshaw holds the record for surfing the biggest wave, an 85-footer at Waimea Bay, Hawaii, on January 20, 1988. Giant waves break as far as two miles from shore so surfers like Ken usually get towed out from shore on Jet-Skis. Some even drop in from a helicopter!

This surfer is taking a giant wave in the Big Wave Invitational surfing championship in Waimea Bay, Hawaii, in 2004.

DAUNTLESS DOLPHIN

On August 20, 2000, Davide Ceci was boating with his father, Emanuele Ceci, in the Adriatic Sea near Manfredonia, Italy, when he fell out of the boat. His father was busy steering the boat and didn't see the 14-year-old go overboard. Davide didn't know how to swim; the last thing he saw before sinking beneath the waves was the boat sailing away. Then Davide felt something large push him up to the surface. It was a dolphin. And amazingly, Davide knew this particular dolphin by name. "Felippo" had shown up in the bay two years earlier and had become the unofficial mascot of their seaside community. The boy held on tightly while Felippo chased down Mr. Ceci's boat, then swam alongside until Davide's dad was able to reach down and pull his son to safety.

SCUBA DO!

Sailor, scientist, inventor, explorer, filmmaker, and TV host, Jacques Cousteau made it possible for humans to explore the world under the sea.

How long can you hold your breath underwater? Most people can only hold it for a minute or two. And until 1943, that was the longest most divers could spend under the surface. That's when French naval officer Jacques Cousteau and engineer Emile Gagnan invented a device to let divers breathe underwater for hours. They called it the *aqualung*, and it wasn't long before he started using it to get an "up close" look at the astounding world of undersea life.

The experience changed him forever. A few years later he set out on his research ship, the *Calypso*, to explore the oceans of the world. Cousteau visited every body of water on Earth, from the Arctic Ocean to the Mississippi River. He revealed the amazing beauty of the ocean depths in his award-winning films *The Silent World* and *World Without Sun* and in his 1970s television show, *The Undersea World of Jacques Cousteau*. By the time he died in 1997, Cousteau had done more to teach people about the oceans than anyone who's ever lived. Best of all, he gave all of us the opportunity to become underwater explorers—just like him.

DIVING DOWN

Here's a quick guide to the history of deep sea diving.

2500 BC—A Greek named Scyllis invents the breathing tube. While being held prisoner by the Persians, he discovers their attack plans and jumps overboard. That night, using a reed as a snorkel, he swims underwater from ship to ship and sabotages the Persian fleet.

1535—Guglielmo de Lorena makes the first practical diving bell—an upside-down pot lowered into the water, trapping air that divers can breathe for a short time.

1690—John Lethbridge invents the first "diving suit," an enclosed wooden cylinder with leather sleeves. To everyone's surprise, it works.

1788—John Smeaton makes a *better* diving bell. This one has a hand pump to get fresh air. Within 10 years, his bell is used all over Europe and America.

1837—Augustus Siebe invents the first rubber diving suit sealed to an attached diving helmet. This type of diving suit is still used today.

1865—Two Frenchmen invent the "Aerophore"—an air tank strapped to the diver's back and connected by a mouthpiece. It inspires Jules Verne to include one in his novel, *20,000 Leagues Under the Sea.*

1917—The Mark V Diving Helmet becomes the official diving helmet of the US Navy. (It still is.)

1930—William Beebe sets a depth record of 1,426 feet in a round steel ball called a *bathysphere* attached to a mother ship by a steel cable.

1930—Guy Gilpatric invents rubber goggles. Snorkels and fins are already in use.

1943—Jacques-Yves Cousteau and Emil Gagnan invent the *aqualung*, the first practical SCUBA gear.

1954—Georges Houot and Pierre-Willm take the newly invented *bathyscaphe*, a submarine-like submersible, 13,287 feet under the sea—a new record.

1960—Jacques Piccard and Don Walsh pilot the bathyscaphe *Trieste* 35,820 feet into the Mariana Trench. It is the absolute bottom of the ocean, and no one will ever go deeper.

SWIM SCHOOL

You probably know that fish swim in schools. But did you know a group of sharks is called a shiver? Try to match each sea creature with its group.

1. Starfish	**A.** Glide
2. Jellyfish	**B.** Gam
3. Turtles	**C.** Bale
4. Oysters	**D.** Smack
5. Dolphins	**E.** Swarm
6. Seahorses	**F.** Army
7. Eels	**G.** Troubling
8. Whales	**H.** Colony
9. Rainbow Fish	**I.** Herd
10. Crabs	**J.** Party
11. Goldfish	**K.** Bed
12. Sardines	**L.** Cast
13. Herring	**M.** Family
14. Flying fish	**N.** Pod

DID YOU KNOW?

A school of fish can also be called a *shoal*, a *haul*, a *draught*, a *run*, a *catch*, a *flutter*, a *cast*, a *throw*, or a *warp* of fish!

ANSWERS: 1-H, 2-D, 3-C, 4-K, 5-N, 6-I, 7-E, 8-B, 9-J, 10-L, 11-G, 12-M, 13-F, 14-A.

IT'S SLIMY!
IT'S DISGUSTING!
IT'S A HAGFISH!

This slimy eel can tie itself in knots!

Hagfish are the vultures of the sea. They live in the mucky goop that covers the ocean floor, feeding on the bodies of dead fish that sink down from the surface. The way they like to eat the carcasses is truly gross: They crawl inside the body and eat their way out. These primitive fish haven't changed for over 300 million years. Hagfish are nearly blind, have three hearts, no jaws or stomach, and no bones. They are also called *slime eels*, and here's why: When another

predator grabs them, they cover themselves with slime—gobs of it. A hagfish can crank out a gallon of the stuff in seconds. Then it ties itself in a knot, which usually lets it slip out of the predator's grip. Hagfish also use the knot trick to clean off their slime once they're free. And if that doesn't do the trick—they sneeze!

REAL MONSTERS?

Meet Oregon's most famous sea serpents.

Fishermen have been sighting sea serpents off the Oregon coast for more than 100 years. Two of them have become so well known that they have their own names: Colossal Claude and Marvin the Monster.

COLOSSAL CLAUDE

This monster was first seen in 1934 swimming near the mouth of the Columbia River. Eyewitness L.A. Larson described it as "eight feet long, with a big round body, a mean-looking tail, and an evil, snaky head." Three years later, Claude was spotted again by another person, who described the creature as being a long, tan-colored, hairy monster with a head like a horse. Other fishermen saw Claude, too, but they were reluctant to get too close for fear the beast would flip over their boats. But the schooner *Arpo* sailed within a few feet and got a good look at the monster as it snatched a big halibut off the boat's fishing line. According to Captain Chris Anderson, the monster had "glassy eyes, and a head like a camel." Even odder was the fact that Colossal Claude seemed to be covered in *fur*.

MARVIN THE MONSTER

When this creature made its first appearance in 1963, it scared the wetsuits off some oil company divers exploring an offshore canyon. Fortunately, the divers were able to film the 15-foot-long monster and show the movie to marine biologists at universities in California, Washington, and Texas. Marvin the Monster has popped up many times since then, and film of him swimming around underwater has been shown on television. But scientists still have no idea what kind of creature Marvin —or Claude, for that matter—might be.

STOP THAT LOBSTER!

*It's not a good idea to eat the claw
that saved your wallet...*

A LUCKY CATCH

One hot August evening in 2006, Paul Westlake of Milehouse, England, decided to jump into the ocean to cool off. When he got out, Paul realized that he'd lost his wallet somewhere in the water. It was too dark to dive down to find it, so he figured it was gone forever.

A few days later, a local diver spotted a lobster scurrying along the ocean bottom...carrying a wallet in one of its claws. The diver caught the lobster (and the wallet), and went home. That night, over a delicious lobster dinner, he thumbed through the contents of the wallet and found a hair salon appointment card for Paul Westlake. When he called the next day, the hair stylist thought it was a prank. But when the diver brought the wallet by, the salon notified Paul, who was soon reunited with his soggy wallet. Paul never got to thank the diver (he had walked away without identifying himself), and he felt awful when he found out the lobster had been eaten. "I have never eaten a lobster," he said, "and now I never will."

RUBBER DUCKIES OVERBOARD!

In 1992 there was a shipping accident that spilled 29,000 rubber ducks and other bath toys into the middle of the Pacific Ocean. The little yellow ducks floated on the ocean for almost a year, just going with the flow…until one day a few thousand washed up on the shores of Alaska. Many more continued their journey north through the Bering Straits and were frozen in the Arctic icepack. By 2003—11 years later—these frozen adventurers had finally made their way across the Pole to the North Atlantic and were spotted bobbing merrily off beaches from Maine to Massachusetts.

DAVY JONES' LOCKER

Uncle John wants to know—who the heck is Davy Jones?

For centuries, when a sailor was drowned at sea, sailors would say, "He's gone to Davy Jones' Locker," meaning he was buried at the bottom of the sea. But where did the phrase come from? The first written reference to Davy Jones was in the 1751 novel *The Adventures of Peregrine Pickle*, where he was described as a real sea devil with saucer-like eyes, three rows of teeth, horns, a tail, and blue smoke coming out of his nose. The 2006 movie *Pirates of the Caribbean: Dead Man's Chest* presented Davy Jones as an evil mutant mix of human and octopus. But how did he get the name Davy Jones? One theory says "Davy" comes from St. David, the patron saint of sailors, and "Jones" is from Jonah, the Biblical seaman who got swallowed by a whale, and whose name still means bad luck to sailors.

But there's another legend. According to this story, Davy Jones was a 16th century Welsh innkeeper with a nasty side business: He would get sailors so drunk that they'd pass out. Then he'd stick them in his ale locker (a room used to store barrels of ale) until some friends arrived with a cart to haul the unconscious sailors to the nearest ship that was short a few crewmen. Jones got a tidy fee for each "delivery." As for the drunken sailor, he'd wake up when the ship was far out to sea, with a headache…and the shock of his life.

HERE BE TREASURE!

Tales of pirate gold, lost and found...

DOUBLE TROUBLE. Ever dream of finding buried pirate booty? Travel to the Costa Rican island of Cocos and you may get a two-for-one. In 1818, somewhere in the island's tree-covered hills, Benito "Bloody Sword" Bonito buried a load of Spanish gold worth $300 million. In 1820 another pirate, William Thompson, hijacked the legendary Treasure of Lima (the wealth of more than 50 churches in the Peruvian capital), and stashed it on Cocos. Since then, hundreds of treasure hunters have scoured the island—including President Franklin Roosevelt—but no one has ever found either hoard.

HAPPY ENDING? Captain "Black Sam" Bellamy's ship, the *Whydah*, sank off the coast of New England in 1717. Along with the 143 pirates who drowned was a fortune in gold and silver. Deep-sea diver Barty Clifford searched for 15 years without success, but in 1984 he finally found the ship. So far, more than 100,000 treasure items, including chests of gold and silver doubloons, have been pulled from the wreck of the *Whydah*. Clifford is certain that most of the treasure is still lost in the sand, waiting to be found.

BATTLE, BARF, AND BULLION

Whale vomit is as rare as gold,
and worth a whole lot more!

THE BATTLE

Somewhere down deep in the ocean, two of the world's largest predators will face each other today in a battle of life and death. On one side is the bull sperm whale—60 feet long, 65 tons, with a mouthful of razor-sharp teeth and a nasty attitude. A sperm whale can hold its breath up to two hours while it dives more than a mile below the surface to hunt for its favorite food—the giant squid. The monster squid are as big as the whales that hunt them. With a sharp beak, sucker-lined arms, and two whip-like feeding tentacles, a giant squid is no pushover. No one has ever witnessed a fight

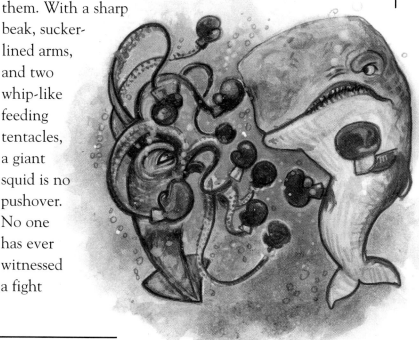

between these deep-sea behemoths, but battle scars are visible on the whales when they surface—deep gashes from the beaks, and round welts left by the suckers. Sometimes the squid escapes, disappearing behind a cloud of dark ink. If the whale wins, it swallows the squid whole. But the squid gets revenge: Its beak is indigestible, which irritates the whale's stomach until sooner or later it barfs it out.

THE BARF

For most creatures, that would be the end of the story. But not the sperm whale. The black gooey vomit drifts along the ocean currents, soaking up the sun. Over time it hardens into a sweet-smelling, waxy lump known as *ambergris*. Or, as sailors have long called it, "floating gold."

THE BULLION

Ambergris has been prized for thousands of years. The Chinese thought it came from sleeping dragons drooling on sunny seashore rocks, so they called it "dragon's spittle perfume." The Dutch and English used to breakfast on ambergris and eggs. It has been used as medicine, a spice for food and wine and, most significantly, as an ingredient in making fine perfume. It's been cut up into round balls, polished, and worn as "whale pearls." Ambergris is so valuable that just one gram of it (.035 of an ounce) can fetch up to $20. However, it comes in so many different colors, shapes, and textures that most beachcombers don't know real ambergris when they find it.

UNCLE JOHN'S AMBERGRIS TEST

In case you're not sure whether to show that weird goop you found on the beach to your science teacher...

WHAT YOU'LL NEED

1 batch of possible whale barf found on beach

1 needle, 1 match, and 1 candle (and adult supervision)

HOW TO DO IT

1. Heat the needle

2. Briefly touch the whale barf with the hot needle.

3. Real ambergris will melt instantly. A black oily residue will ooze from the pricked spot, and a puff of musky-smelling smoke will appear.

Dorothy Ferreira of Long Island, New York, got this piece of (maybe) ambergris as a gift in 2006. She's having it tested to see if it's the real thing. If it is, it may be worth $18,000!

HEY, LET GO OF MY BOAT!

The skies were clear, the wind crisp. Olivier de Kersauson's sleek racing boat was speeding through the deep ocean off the island of Madeira in the South Atlantic. The veteran French sailor and his crew were just beginning an around-the-world race to win the prestigious Jules Verne Trophy, when all at once they got the surprise of their lives. De Kersauson was below deck when the hull shuddered and the boat slowed down abruptly. Looking out the porthole, he saw a giant tentacle thicker than his leg. Rushing up on deck, he found two other tentacles wrapped around the rudder. A giant squid 24 feet long had grabbed hold of the yacht and wouldn't let go. Luckily for de Kersauson, he didn't have to fight off the monster—as soon as the boat came to a stop, the giant squid released the boat and slid beneath the waves. "We didn't have anything to scare off this beast, so I don't know what we would have done if it hadn't let go," de Kersauson said later. "We weren't going to attack it with our penknives."

"HA! YOU MISSED ME!"

Diving for abalone—a shellfish prized for its delicate flavor—isn't the easiest job in the world. The water is cold and murky, and predators prowl the shadows. Since abalone divers stay underwater for six or seven hours at a stretch, they have to wear lead-weighted vests to stay submerged. For one Australian diver, that vest saved his life.

Eric Nerhus was diving off New South Wales, Australia, in 2007 when a 10-foot great white shark decided to eat him—head first. The bite crushed Eric's mask and broke his nose, but what came next was worse. Within seconds, his head and shoulders were completely inside the shark's throat. But Eric had no intention of being shark lunch. A black belt in karate, he used his free arm to punch at the shark's eyes and gills until it spit him out. But it was his vest that saved his life—it protected him from the shark's teeth like a coat of armor. Lucky Eric walked away with cuts and scrapes, and bite marks on his chest. (The vest had to be thrown away.)

S. O. S.

Ten things you can do to Save Our Seas.

It's only recently that humans have come to understand how much we need a healthy ocean to survive. The ocean makes most of the oxygen we breathe. It cleans the water we drink. It gives us food and even medicine. But we've haven't taken good care of it—we dump our garbage into it, and we've fished some species to near-extinction, destroying coral reefs in the process. Today the ocean is in trouble. But if we work together, we can help stop the damage we've done…and we have to start right away.

AT THE BEACH

1. Keep the ocean clean. Take your trash home with you, even if there's a trashcan on the beach.

2. Protect the sand dunes. Don't walk or play on the dunes. They help prevent erosion.

3. Protect the wildlife. Avoid nesting areas, and don't bother or chase sea birds or animals.

4. Protect the reefs. Reefs are *very* fragile. Just one touch can harm a reef—walking on one can kill it.

5. Fish smart. Catch what you can eat and release the rest. Take all fishing lines and nets home with you, even the broken ones. Birds and fish can get tangled in them and die.

AT HOME

6. Don't let go of that balloon! Sea turtles mistake balloons (and plastic bags) for their favorite food, jellyfish, which can be a fatal mistake.

7. Shop smart. Only buy things that you really want or need. The less stuff we throw away, the less stuff that gets dumped in the ocean.

8. Eat sustainable food. Eat fish and shellfish caught or farmed in ways that support the oceans in the long-term. Go organic—pesticides and fertilizers from traditional farming are poisoning the ocean.

9. Reduce your greenhouse gas footprint. When you walk, ride your bike, turn off the lights, and recycle, you produce fewer greenhouse gasses. That helps reduce global warming, and helps keep the oceans at temperatures that support wildlife.

10. Learn everything you can about the ocean. Share what you've learned with your friends. They might be inspired to help protect the ocean, too.

And...on June 8th, celebrate World Ocean Day.

POLAR OPPOSITES

Some chillin' facts...

NORTH POLE

- The Arctic is a frozen ocean surrounded by continents.

- The Arctic is named after the Big Dipper constellation, also know as the Great Bear. In Greek, both are called called *Arktikos*.

- The pack ice in the Arctic Ocean is an average of 10–12 feet thick.

- Polar bears, walruses, beluga, and narwhals are found only in the Arctic.

- Trees and shrubs grow along the southern edges of the Arctic.

- Lots of land animals live in the Arctic—arctic foxes, rabbits, caribou elk, and reindeer, to name a few.

- Even if all the ice in the Arctic Ocean melted, the oceans wouldn't rise. That's because ice floats on the ocean and displaces its weight in seawater. Think of a full glass of iced tea: When the ice cubes melt, does the level rise? No, it stays the same (unless, of course, you've been drinking the tea).

POLAR OPPOSITES

...to help you keep your poles straight.

SOUTH POLE

- The Antarctic is a continent surrounded by ocean.

- The word *Antarctic* means "opposite of Arctic."

- The ice sheets covering the continent of Antarctica have an average depth of 1.5 miles.

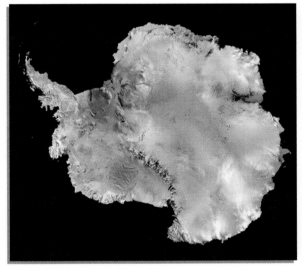

The continent of Antarctica, seen from space.

- Emperor, Adelie, Chinstrap, and Gentoo penguins live only in the Antarctic.

- No trees or bushes grow in the Antarctic— only moss, algae, and lichens. Because it's so cold, some plants actually grow *inside* the rocks.

- The only land animals that live in the Antarctic are midges, mites, ticks, and nematode worms.

- Because Antarctica is a continent, if all of its ice sheets melted, the ice would flow off the land into the sea. That would cause the ocean to rise by 200 feet.

SEALS

Go ahead...clap your flippers and bark.

WHAT HAS A TORPEDO-SHAPED BODY, 4 FLIPPERS, AND NO EARS?

You guessed it—a seal. Its torpedo-like body allows it to zip through the water at speeds of up to 25 mph, and dive down 1,000 feet. Its two front flippers have claws and are used for steering; the rear flippers are its propellers.

WHAT'S THE BIGGEST SEAL?

It's the elephant seal, of course, which can weigh as much as 5,000 pounds.

WHAT'S THE SMALLEST SEAL?

An adult ringed seal tips the scales at only 110 pounds.

WHAT DO SEALS LIKE TO EAT?

Krill, squid, and fish—but not necessarily in that order.

WHERE DO SEALS LIVE?

Anywhere they want to. Really. Seals live in all of the oceans of the world. They even pop up in freshwater lakes, such as Lake Baikal in Russia. But the majority can be found near Antarctica and the Arctic Circle.

HOW MANY KINDS OF SEALS ARE THERE?

There are 18 seal species, which include the harbor seal, the bearded seal, the crabeater seal, the harp seal, the spotted seal, and the hooded seal. There used to be a 19th species—the Caribbean monk seal—but it was last seen in 1952. It's now thought to be extinct.

WHAT IS THE MOST FEROCIOUS SEAL?

The leopard seal wins this award. A predator that gets its name from its black spots, it can grow to be 12 feet long. It has long, sharp teeth and a head that looks like a reptile's. A leopard seal likes to lie in wait under the ice in Antarctica for its dinner to come along. Then it bursts out of the water, snapping up penguins, smaller seals, and sometimes taking a bite at a polar explorer or two.

FOLLOW THAT FIN!

For more than 20 years, a dolphin named Pelorus Jack guided sailing ships through dangerous waters.

Hundreds of shipwrecks litter the sea floor between New Zealand's North and South Islands, victims of the treacherous rocks and swirling currents of a narrow channel known as the French Pass. So when the sailing ship *Brindle* entered the channel in 1888, the sailors were understandably alarmed when they heard a shout from a crew member. Had they run aground? No, but to their amazement, they saw a Risso's dolphin swimming alongside the ship.

GOING MY WAY?

Risso's are open-ocean dolphins that prefer the company of their own pod, not people. To see one at all was rare; to see one near a ship was very unusual. What was even more odd was the dolphin's behavior: It wasn't playing in the bow wake, as dolphins commonly do. Instead, it seemed to be *leading* the ship through the channel.

And when the *Brindle* set out on its return trip, the dolphin was waiting at the mouth of the channel, ready to guide the ship safely back. The grateful sailors nick-named their finny guide Pelorus Jack, after the *pelorus*, a compass used to get one's bearings on the open ocean.

For the next 24 years, Pelorus Jack guided ships safely through the channel. The dolphin was so reliable that ships would wait for him to appear before going forward.

The dolphin's fame grew and people flocked to see him, including authors Rudyard Kipling and Mark Twain. Then in 1904, a drunken passenger on a ship called the *Penguin* shot the dolphin. Pelorus Jack swam away, leaving a trail of blood behind him. No one knew if Jack was alive or dead. Two weeks later, the dolphin reappeared and took up his usual post. But Jack never led the *Penguin* through the channel again. The shooting incident caused an outrage, and a law was passed making it illegal to shoot a dolphin in New Zealand waters.

One of the few existing photos of Jack.

GOODBYE, OLD FRIEND

Pelorus Jack guided his last ship on April 12, 1912. He disappeared shortly after that, and probably died of old age. Grateful New Zealanders declared a day of national mourning to honor him.

Five years after the shooting incident, on February 12, 1909, the *Penguin* sank on the rocks of French Pass. It was the only ship lost in the channel during Pelorus Jack's career.

FUNGHI

*No, not a mushroom, but the
famous Dolphin of Dingle.*

Funghi is a bottlenose dolphin who swam into the Bay of Dingle one day—and never left. Since 1983, Funghi has entertained visitors to Dingle, a quaint town on the west coast of Ireland, every day of the week, escorting boats in and out of the harbor. He surfs the bow wakes of the boats, and even lets swimmers come up and play with him. The dolphin's presence has become so predictable that a huge tourist industry has grown up around him, making Funghi famous all over the world.

LONG-ARMED RESCUE

Can't reach that hard-to-get spot?
Call the world's tallest man!

On December 13, 2006, veterinarians at Royal Jidi Ocean World in Fushon, China, found themselves facing a tricky problem: Two mischievous dolphins had swallowed some large pieces of plastic that had been left by their pool. The vet couldn't anesthetize them and remove the objects surgically because, unlike most animals, dolphins can't breathe if they're not awake.

The vet tried to pull out the plastic pieces by reaching down the dolphins' throats, but his arm was too short. They needed someone with a *really* long arm. Enter Bao Xishun, the World's Tallest Man. According to the *Guinness Book of Records*, he's 7 feet, 8 inches tall. His arms are 3 feet, 4 inches long—long enough to reach down and pull out the dangerous pieces of plastic.

Each dolphin was held down by a dozen keepers, and towels were wrapped around their jaws to keep the dolphins' sharp teeth from scratching Bao's arm. The operation was over in seconds. Good thing, too, because the plastic had been in the dolphins' stomachs for over two weeks. The vets said they would have died soon if the long-armed surgery hadn't worked!

GENTLE GIANTS

These huge sharks are the "vacuum cleaners" of the sea!

Some of the largest fish live by eating the smallest food. Meet the giant sharks: These easy-going guys have nothing in common with their fiercer cousins. They're "filter feeders"—they swim along with their mouths wide open, scooping up huge amounts of water which they strain through long bristles called *gill rakers*. They flush out the water and keep the stuff they like: plankton, fish eggs, and tiny shrimp known as *krill*.

BASKING SHARK

The basking shark is the world's second largest fish—it can grow up to 33 feet long and weigh 8,000 pounds.

The basking shark also has hundreds of tiny teeth inside its mouth... but they're of little or no use. These filter-feeders hang out near the surface of the ocean, either alone or in schools of up to 100 sharks.

WHALE SHARK

Whale sharks are the world's biggest fish. They can grow up to 46 feet long and weigh more than 47,000 pounds. (Remember, they're not whales—they're *fish*.) The whale shark has 3,000 teeth in its cavernous mouth, but the teeth are tiny and harmless. Whale sharks are found in all the warm oceans of the world.

MEGAMOUTH

The first megamouth shark was discovered in Hawaii in 1976. Since then, only 38 more have been seen, making the megamouth one of the rarest sharks in the world. This weird-looking creature has an oversized head with big rubbery lips and a huge mouth, lined with 50 rows of tiny teeth. The largest megamouth on record was 16 feet long and weighed 2,205 pounds.

SHARK JOKES

For those of you who like a little bite in your humor...

Q: *What happens when you cross a great white shark with a cow?*
A: I don't know—but whatever you do, don't milk it.

Q: *What does a shark eat with peanut butter?*
A: Jellyfish.

Q: *Why do sharks swim only in saltwater?*
A: Because pepper water would make them sneeze.

Q: *What happened to the shark who swallowed a bunch of keys?*
A: He got lockjaw.

Q: *How can you tell a boy shark from a girl shark?*
A: You give it a fish. If *he* eats it, it's a boy...if *she* eats it, it's a girl.

Q: *Why don't sharks eat clowns?*
A: They taste funny.

Q: *What do you get from a bad-tempered shark?*
A: As far away as possible!

Q: *Where do fish go when they want to borrow money?*
A: A loan shark.

Q: *What do you get when you cross a big fish with an electric wire?*
A: An electric shark.

MESSAGE IN A BOTTLE

You never know what you'll find washed up on shore.

LUCKY FIND

The most incredible "message in a bottle" story of all time took place in San Francisco in 1949. Jack Wurm was having a rough time: He'd lost his job and run out of money. Hopeless and depressed, he took a walk along the beach, trying to figure out what to do next. Then he noticed a bottle with a piece of paper in it sticking out of the sand. He picked it up and pried off

the cork. What he found inside was almost too good to be true—a signed will that read, "I leave my entire estate to the lucky person who finds this bottle." The will belonged to the late Daisy Singer Alexander, heiress to the Singer sewing machine fortune. She had thrown the bottle in the Thames River in England 12 years earlier. The bottle and the will had drifted all the way around the world to San Francisco, and to Jack Wurm—who became a millionaire overnight!

GUESS WHO?

Some fish do whatever they can to not look like a fish.

LEAFY SEA DRAGON

These relatives of the
sea horse look like
floating pieces of sea-
weed—a perfect dis-
guise for hiding among
the patches of kelp-
covered rocks where
they make their home
in cool waters off the

coast of Australia. Their mouths work like a drinking
straw: When the tiny shrimp they like to eat swim by,
leafy sea dragons slurp them up like a milk shake.

TASSELED WOBBEGONG

This bizarre-looking creature likes to bury its flattened
body against the sea floor and wait for lunch to swim by.
Its amazing camouflage of patterns and colors make it

look like leftover shag
carpet...which is why
it's also called a carpet
shark. This native of the
South Pacific hides out
in caves, or rests on
coral reefs down to
depths of 130 feet.

Now you see him...

BIG BLUE (DAY) OCTOPUS

Say hello to one of the supreme masters of sea disguise. Not only can a big blue octopus change color, it can alter the texture of its skin to look just like the reef rock it lives on. That's a great survival skill for a creature that hunts in broad daylight. While diving off the coast of Hawaii, one marine biologist watched a big blue change its look 1,000 times in seven hours.

...now you don't!

IT WAS TH-I-I-I-S BIG!

More of the biggest sea creatures ever found.

• The largest *leatherback turtle* ever recorded was 10 feet from tip to tail, and weighed in at 2,019 pounds.

• A *trumpet conch* collected in 1979 off the coast of Australia was 30 inches long and 40 inches around. The snail inside it weighed 40 pounds, making it the largest marine snail on record.

• The largest *sea star* was found in the North Pacific Ocean. It weighed 11 pounds and was nearly 38 inches in diameter.

• The largest *clam* ever collected was taken in 1917 from Australia's Great Barrier Reef. It was 49 inches long and weighed 579 pounds. An even bigger clam was discovered in 1965, measuring 53 inches in length. But the divers left it on the reef to keep on growing!

• In 1934 a Filipino diver found a huge *pearl* 10 inches in diameter and weighing 14 pounds. Today the pearl, now known as the Pearl of Lao-tze, is worth $40 million.

SEA SQUIRT

Talk about losing your mind. This guy eats his own brain!

Sea squirts are *tunicates*—animals made up of a simple tube, which they use as a siphon to suck in passing plankton. Unlike worms and jellyfish, sea squirts have a backbone, which makes them vertebrates, just like us. In fact, scientists think sea squirts may have been one of the first vertebrates to exist on the planet. In the early stages of its development, a sea squirt embryo looks much like any other vertebrate's embryo, whether it's a rat, fish, lion, or human. And baby sea squirts are born with a brain, just like people. So you could say that the sea squirt is our distant cousin.

The sea squirt does something unique in the sea world. A baby sea squirt uses its brain to pick out a permanent place to live. Once it's found a spot of rock to attach itself to, it doesn't need that brain anymore—so the sea squirt eats it. Really. It absorbs its simple brain back into its body and goes on merrily with its simple life— sucking in, blowing out, sucking in, blowing out…

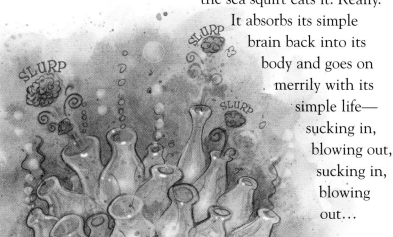

BIG MOUTHS

What do these three fish have in common? They can all swallow prey larger than themselves.

GULPER EEL

This deep-sea fish isn't much more than a giant mouth  with a tail so long that it sometimes gets tied in knots. The average gulper is about two feet long, although some can grow to six feet. Their huge mouths are hinged loosely so they can open them wide like a net. This lets them "gulp" animals much larger than themselves. Conveniently, a gulper's stomach stretches out to handle a "biggie size" meal.

Gulpers live way down deep in the ocean, anywhere from 3,000–10,000 feet.

HAIRY ANGLER

The *hairy angler* was only recently discovered when one drifted into range of a BBC camera during the filming of the documentary *The Blue Planet* in 2003. The hairy angler's Latin name is *Caulophryne polynema*, which means "stalked toad with many filaments"—a good description of this peculiar fish. Its beach ball-sized body is covered in long antennae called *neuromasts* which pick out the movements of any prey foolish enough to come close to its mouth, which is full of fanged teeth. Like the gulper eel, it can loosen its jaws to swallow prey bigger than it is, and digest them in its expandable stomach. Hairy anglers haunt the black waters of the Atlantic Ocean down to 8,000 feet.

FANGTOOTH

The *fangtooth*'s teeth are so big that it can't close its mouth. In fact, it has the largest teeth of any fish in the ocean its size. So it's a good thing this guy is only six inches long. Also called an ogrefish, the fangtooth's squat body is covered with small prickly scales. This is a tough critter: Able to withstand incredible pressures and near-freezing temperatures, the fangtooth can be found all over the world at incredible depths of down to 16,000 feet.

THE SALTY SEA

It's big. It's wet. And you can't drink it.

Why do lakes and rivers have fresh water, while the ocean has salty water? Doesn't all that fresh river water flow right into the ocean? Yes, but on its way to the ocean, that water sucks tons of minerals and chemicals out of the land. By the time it enters the big blue sea, it's full of iron, calcium, magnesium, potassium, silica, nitrate, chloride and…sodium (salt). When this mineral-packed water meets the ocean, the sea life makes good use of it. Plankton use the silica to make their shells. Shrimp, lobsters, and crabs use the calcium to make their claws and armor. Lots of sea creatures use *some* of the minerals in the water, but *none* use sodium, so it stays in the water.

So how much salt is in the ocean? Four billion tons of it run into the ocean each year. For every ton of seawater, there's about 70 pounds of salt mixed in. Some seawater is saltier than others. The Red Sea is the saltiest because it lies in a hot, dry region, between Egypt and Saudi Arabia, where the intense heat causes evaporation; as more water is drawn into the atmosphere, more salt is left behind. The Arctic Ocean is the least salty for the same reason. The colder the ocean air, the less evaporation and the less salt.

SNOT BALLS!

How do creatures at the bottom of the sea get food?

There's a mystery that's puzzled marine biologists for years. They knew that the ocean bottom is crawling with creatures who feed on sediment that settles down to the ocean floor. But they also knew that the sediment contained barely half the food needed to support the population of bottom creatures. So where do those bottom feeders get the rest of their food?

The answer lies near the surface, where little animals called *giant larvaceans* make homes for themselves out of their own mucus. The tadpole-sized creatures spin a mucus web about three feet wide, and hide in the middle of it while it snags their food for them. The web works for about 24 hours before it gets clogged. Then the larvacean jumps ship and starts spinning a new web. The old web sinks all the way to the bottom of the sea, picking up little animals and bits of algae on the way. When these glops of snotty goop finally hit the bottom, the creatures down there gobble them up. And scientists believe these "sinkers" account for half the food on the ocean floor!

THAR' SHE BLOWS!

Whew! Gotta cut down on the plankton!

Did you know that whales fart? It's true! Like humans, they are mammals, so scientists have long figured that whales would pass gas just like every other animal in the world. Now there's proof. Marine biologists in the Antarctic were tracking Minke whales (a relatively small whale, weighing about 5,000 pounds and is 25 feet long) when one of them (a whale, that is) cut a big one. The bubble was more than six feet in diameter when it popped up at the surface near the bow of the ship. The stench was so bad that the scientists frantically ran to the back of the ship to get away.

Now, what Uncle John wants to know is—who pulled the whale's flipper?

GHOST SHIPS

The ocean is huge. Ships are tiny.
Sometimes they get lost...forever.

⚓ THE *MARY CELESTE*

There were 10 people on board the *Mary Celeste* when the 103-foot sailing freighter left New York harbor on November 7, 1872. Captain Ben Briggs, his wife, his two-year-old daughter, and a crew of seven were bound for Genoa, Italy, carrying a cargo of rubbing alcohol. A month later another ship, the *Dei Gratia*, spotted the *Mary Celeste* drifting near the Azores, several hundred miles off the coast of Portugal. When the crew boarded the ship, they found it deserted. There was no sign of a struggle or evidence of any emergency. The kitchen and living quarters were all neatly stowed away. The captain's logbook was open on his desk, with the last entry dated from a week before. It was as if everyone on board had just gotten up and walked off the ship. No trace of Captain Briggs, his family, or the crew was ever found.

⚓ THE *OCTAVIA*

The whaling ship *Herald* was sailing off the coast of Greenland in 1775 when it spotted a derelict ship floating among the icebergs. The whalers promptly sent a boat and crew over to see what had happened. There they found the *Octavia*'s crew below deck—frozen solid and perfectly preserved. The captain was still at his table in his cabin, hunched over his logbook, his pen still in his hand. Afraid that the sailors had died of a plague, the whalers hurried back to their own ship, taking only the *Octavia's* logbook to prove they'd seen the vessel. The last entry in the logbook was dated 1762, which meant that the *Octavia* had been drifting around the Arctic Ocean for 13 years!

⚓ THE *OURANG MEDAN*

Late in July 1947, an American freighter named the *Silver Star* was navigating the Strait of Malacca off the coast of Indonesia when its radioman picked up frantic distress signals from the Dutch freighter *Ourang Medan*. The badly garbled messages rambled about the captain and crew having died mysteriously. There was a burst of gibberish in Morse code, followed by an ominous, "I die." Then the signals stopped. It took the *Silver Star* several hours to reach the *Ourang Medan*. When a boarding party was sent over to investigate, they found a truly ghastly sight: The crew and officers lay in grotesque positions, their eyes wide open, arms thrown out to the sides, looks of terror gripping their dead faces. The ship's dog was dead, too, its teeth bared as if threatened by some unknown menace. Weirdest of all was the sudden chill the rescue team felt while exploring the boiler room—even though the outside temperature was over 100° F. The captain of the *Silver Star* decided to tow the *Ourang Medan* to the nearest port. While the crew was attaching tow lines, smoke began to pour out of the ghost ship. The *Silver Star* barely had time to cut the lines and pull a safe distance away before the *Ourang Medan* blew up and sank.

OFF THE DEEP END

Q: *What happens when you throw a red rock into the Black Sea?*

A: It sinks.

Q: *What happens when you throw a green rock into the Red Sea?*

A: It gets wet.

Mom: Did you give the goldfish fresh water today?

Kid: No, they haven't finished the water I gave them yesterday.

Q: *What do sea monsters eat?*

A: Fish and ships.

Q: *Where do ghosts swim in North America?*

A: In Lake Erie.

Q: *What do you get when you graduate from scuba diving school?*

A: A deep-loma.

GNARLY TEETH— THE QUIZ!

Only one answer to each description is a real animal. The others are all phonies. Can you guess the real one?

1. This creature's nose is lined with long, pointed teeth. When it swims into a school of fish, it whips its snout around like a samurai sword, slashing fish left and right. If something good to eat is buried in the sand, it uses its nose like a rake to get at it.

a) Clam-rake shark   c) Spear shark

b) Sawshark   d) Samurai shark

2. It swims with its mouth slightly open, so it can breathe. On the hunt, it locks onto its target like a streamlined torpedo. This predator has 3,000 teeth in seven rows in its mouth. When a tooth breaks off, the one behind it moves forward and takes its place.

a) Torpedo shark   c) Great white shark

b) Mega-toothed shark   d) Sandpaper shark

3. This animal looks like it has a jousting lance attached to its head. The lance is actually a long, spiraled tooth. The animal is often seen floating on its back, its tusk pointing up at the sky. In medieval times, its tusks were sold as unicorn horns.

a) Unicorn whale   c) Spiraled-tusked whale

b) King Arthur's whale   d) Narwhal

Answers on next page. →

ANSWERS

1–b) The **sawshark** is actually a ray. Like other sharks and rays, it has special receptors on its snout that help it detect tiny electrical impulses of live prey. It's not a danger to humans—unless you happen to get in the way of its nasty sharp nose.

2–c) The **great white shark**'s teeth are made for grab-

bing and tearing. But these teeth are more sensitive than your fingertips. That's why great white sharks "mouth" their prey first, to see if it's a tasty enough to eat. But the taste-test can be bad news for most animals: Even if the great white decides not to take a second bite, the "mouthing" is often fatal.

3–d) The **narwhal**'s mysterious tusk (its left front tooth, actually) is the only spiraled tusk in nature. And, unlike most teeth, it's soft on the outside and hard on the inside. It is so sensitive that the narwhal may be able to detect changes in weather —which is important when you live in the icy waters of the Arctic Ocean.

AMAZING JOURNEY

When Cassandra Villanueve boarded the ferryboat *Aloha* on June 2, 1974, she thought it would be just another ho-hum crossing between the Philippine islands. But 600 miles south of Manila, the *Aloha* caught fire and sank. In the confusion, Mrs. Villanueve fell overboard. She drifted in the rough seas for 12 hours (thankfully, she'd had time to put on a life jacket). When help arrived, it came in the form of a giant sea turtle! The turtle dove down and came up beneath Mrs. Villanueve, lifting her straight out of the water, and began to swim with her on its back. Soon a much smaller turtle climbed onto the turtle's back beside Mrs. Villanueve. It seems the little turtle had decided Mrs. Villanueve had to stay awake, because whenever she dozed off, it nipped her on the back. Two days the later, a Philippine navy ship found them. When the sailors pulled Mrs. Villanueve onto a rescue boat, the sea turtles slipped beneath the waves and disappeared.

TURTLE TIMES

*Fascinating facts about one of
the world's great swimmers.*

● Sea turtles have been swimming in the oceans since the time of the dinosaurs—around 75 million years.

● The *leatherback turtle* is the fastest swimmer. They've been timed at a speed of 22 miles per hour!

● Sea turtles have an excellent sense of time and direction. Scientists think they use the Earth's magnetic field to navigate thousands of miles across the ocean.

● Sea turtles can see very well under water, but out of the water their vision is blurry and nearsighted.

● Unlike land turtles, sea turtles cannot pull their heads and flippers into their shells for protection.

● When baby sea turtles first enter the water, a "swim frenzy" takes over. They will swim nonstop for 24 to 48 hours to get to deeper, safer water.

● Scientists call the first year of a baby sea turtle's life "the lost year" because they are rarely seen during that time.

● Of every 1,000 turtle eggs buried in the sand, only 800 will hatch. Of those 800, only 400 will survive the dangerous run to the ocean. Of those 400, only 200 will live for more than two years, and only *one* will survive the hazards of the sea to become an adult. That turtle can expect to live from 30 to 70 years.

● Once they enter the water, male sea turtles never

leave the sea. (Females return to the beach where they were born to lay their eggs.)

• Some turtles can actually breathe through their butts. All turtles have a hole between their back legs called a *cloaca* that they use to get rid of poop and pee, as well as lay their eggs. Some small turtles suck in air through their *cloaca* and save it in little air sacs. The Fitzroy River turtle of Australia gets almost two-thirds of its air this way.

MORE DOLPHIN FACTS

➤ Dolphins love to play. Favorite games? Blowing bubbles, tag, and toss-the-seaweed.

➤ Dolphins are closely related to cows, pigs, and deer.

➤ A dolphin's skin feels like rubber.

➤ A bottlenose dolphin replaces its top layer of skin every two hours.

➤ Dolphins can dive down 1,000 feet under the ocean and come right back up. If a human diver did that, the sudden change in water pressure would kill him.

➤ A dolphin can propel itself through the water at more than 24 mph. A human needs a boat to go that fast.

➤ Dolphins use *echolocation* to "see" in murky water. By listening to the echoes of their clicks, dolphins can identify the size and location of objects they can't see with their eyes.

THE LOST WORLD

People have been looking for the lost continent of Atlantis for 2,000 years—but did it ever really exist?

THE LEGEND

About 12,000 years ago, according to some stories, a great civilization called Atlantis sprang up on an island continent in the western ocean. The Atlanteans were light-years ahead of other humans, and their advanced technology made them the masters of the world. They built great temples and monuments in their dazzling city. Nothing seemed beyond the reach of their immense power. Then suddenly—they were gone. A violent earthquake ripped open a gaping hole in the ocean. Atlantis sank into the sea and was never seen again.

WHERE'D IT GO?

The Greek philosopher Plato first wrote about this mysterious lost world in 355 B.C. He even described the layout of the city in great detail, included its network of canals. Plato believed Atlantis was located west of the "Pillars of Hercules," the old name for the Strait of Gibraltar. That's the narrow channel that divides Spain from Morocco, and the Mediterranean Sea from the Atlantic Ocean. For centuries, explorers and historians thought the Azores, a series of lonely islands dotting a remote section of the Atlantic Ocean west of Gibraltar, were the remnants of the mountain peaks of Atlantis. But a geological survey of the ocean floor showed it to be covered with a thick layer of undisturbed mud that took millions of years to accumulate. There was no evidence of a sinking landmass or earthquake.

THE MINOAN SOLUTION

A history professor named K.T. Frost came up with a more likely candidate. The island of Crete lies only a few hundred miles south of the Greek mainland in the Aegean Sea. Centuries before Plato's time, it was home to the Minoans, a brilliant civilization that ruled the Mediterranean. Like the Atlanteans, the Minoans were more advanced than their Greek neighbors. They had great palaces filled with beautiful paintings. And like the Atlanteans, the Minoans vanished almost overnight.

A likely spot for the city of Atlantis can be found 10 miles off the coast of Crete on the small island of Santorini. Today Santorini is actually several little islands ringing a central lagoon, but 2,500 years ago it was one big island with a volcano at its center. In the year 1500 B.C.—900 years before Plato's time—that volcano exploded. The explosion caused a tidal wave 100 feet high, which swept over the sea and a mile inland, obliterating the great Minoan civilization in the same way Plato described the end of Atlantis.

THE SEARCH GOES ON

But some experts aren't satisfied with the Minoan theory, since Plato wrote that the fall of Atlantis occurred 9,000 years before his time, not 900. And he was adamant that the continent of Atlantis lay to the *west* of Greece, not to the south like Crete. So explorers continue to scour the oceans of the world for evidence of Atlantis. So far, no one has been able to provide convincing proof that Atlantis was ever more than a figment of Plato's imagination. But that hasn't stopped adventurers from trying. One theory suggests that the great city was indeed in the Atlantic Ocean, but much farther away, in the Bermuda Triangle off the coast of Florida. Others put the lost continent back in the Mediterranean, near the island of Cyprus, or in the North Atlantic, near Ireland. And the most extreme theory says that Atlantis was really on the *other* side of the world...in the South China Sea, off the coast of Vietnam.

FISH CAN FLY?

Not every fish in the sea is a swimmer.

FLYING FISH. The 50 species of flying fish around the world come in many colors and shapes, but they all have one thing in common—huge pectoral (chest) fins. These "wings" let flying fish escape predators by leaping out of the water and gliding for up to 350 feet! They can launch themselves into the air at 30 mph, too, which makes them difficult to catch. Unfortunately, they don't have much control over their landing, so flying fish often wind up stranded on the decks of boats.

MUDSKIPPERS. These little fish (1–3 inches) can't fly, but they can walk. They spend more of their lives out of the water than in it. In fact, they walk faster than they swim. Their pectoral fins work much like legs, which is great for fish that live in tidal areas where the water comes and goes unpredictably. Mudskippers have gills like regular fish, but they can also absorb oxygen right through their skin.

DON'T BITE ME!

The eel with sharp teeth and a bad rep.

Okay, first of all, the *moray eel* is not an eel. Or a sea snake. It's a fish. Two hundred species of morays live in tropical seas around the world. Sometimes they're called the *painted eel* because of the amazing variety of patterns and colors they have as camouflage. Some morays are polka-dotted; others are orange, bright yellow, or even zebra-striped. But unlike other fish, morays don't have scales—they have skin. It's thick and tough and covered with slime.

With its mouthful of sharp teeth, the moray eel looks really nasty. But it's actually a shy, docile creature. It can't see very well, so it would much rather spend its day holed up in a small rocky crevice than venture out in the open to bite off the toes of a nosy diver. So why do morays bare their teeth like they're snarling? They have to keep their mouths open to breathe. But be careful! If you bother one by sticking your hand near its hiding place, you may get a vicious bite. It's not because the moray eel's a meanie, though. It's because you just scared the slime out of it!

GODS OF THE SEA

Confronted with the awesome power of the ocean, ancient people believed there had to be a god behind it.

POSEIDON

Origin: Greece

Background: Poseidon lives in a beautiful palace in the kingdom of Atlantis. He's usually seen with a horse, carrying a three-pronged pitchfork known as a *trident*. It's a good idea not to upset Poseidon—he tends to cause earthquakes when he gets angry. (He's also the god of horses, rivers... and earthquakes.)

ÆGIR

Origin: Scandinavia

Background: Ægir is a giant, and he loves to party. His elaborate banquets are famous among the other Norse gods. Ægir has no problem sinking a boat, and carrying off its cargo and crew to his golden palace at the bottom of the sea. To stay on Ægir's good side, Viking sailors would kill a prisoner as a sacrifice before setting sail.

RYUJIN

Origin: Japan

Background: Ryujin owns the magical Tide Jewels

that control the tides and make tsunamis. He is the dragon god of the sea, but may also appear as a human being. In his huge red and white coral palace on the ocean bottom, human fish are his servants and sea turtles are his personal messengers. One day in Ryujin's palace is equal to 100 years on land.

KANALOA

Origin: Hawaii

Background: Also called the Great Octopus, Kanaloa is magician, a healer, and god of the underworld. He lives in a place known as the "lost islands" and is almost always seen with Kane, the god of the land and the trees, either fishing, sailing, or finding fresh water. Kanaloa always takes the shape of an octopus or squid. Hawaiian fishermen still look to him for protection.

MANANNAN MAC LIR

Origin: Ireland

Background: This god has a cloak of invisibility, and can forecast the weather. Manannan mac Lir is most often seen riding over the waves in his chariot, wearing a helmet of flames. He also owns a magical ship, the *Wave Sweeper*, which doesn't need wind or sails to speed across the ocean.

LEMANJA

Origin: Africa

Background: The Queen of the Sea, and protector of sailors and fishermen, Lemanja is not only beautiful, but compassionate, too. Anyone who dies at sea may live with her in her palace at the bottom of the sea. Sometimes she rises to the surface to listen to the songs sailors sing to her.

FREE WILLY

*The star of three major motion pictures
was an orca named Keiko.*

Keiko was two years old when he was captured by a fisherman off the coast of Iceland and sold to a marine amusement park. Thus began his long career in show business: Keiko performed tricks in Iceland and Canada before he finally ended up at Reino Aventura, an amusement park in Mexico City. The public loved Keiko, but living in a cramped freshwater tank isn't good for an orca. In 1992 Keiko was discovered by Hollywood and starred in the movie *Free Willy*, about a boy who wanted to free a killer whale from a marine theme park. In an art-imitates-life moment, fans of the movie formed the Free Willy/Keiko Foundation to help Keiko escape his miserable life in Mexico City. He was airlifted first to Oregon, and then to Iceland where he swam in salt water and was taught how to hunt live fish like other orcas. When Keiko was finally released into the open waters, he swam 870 miles to the Taknes Fjord in Norway. He died at the ripe old age of 27, free at last.

WOOF! IT'S A WHALE

*The ancestor of today's whales
looked a lot like man's best friend.*

Whales are huge, have no legs, and live in the ocean, right? Well, that's true today, but 50 million years ago, the first whale actually looked more like a dog. It wasn't very big, either—about the size of a wolf. It didn't even live in the ocean. *Pakicetus* (its scientific name) hunted fish along the shores of the shallow seas that covered the Punjab region of Asia. Today the Punjab, which is in India and Pakistan, is almost a desert.

How do scientists know *pakicetus* was a whale? Because of the unusual structure of the ear region of its skull—a shape found only in whales, dolphins, and their ancestors.

THE LARGEST LIVING THING

It's over a thousand miles long...and it's ALIVE!

WHAT IS...

)● ...the largest living organism on the planet?

)● ...one of the Seven Natural Wonders of the World?

)● ...and something so big it can be seen from the International Space Station?

IF YOU GUESSED THE GREAT BARRIER REEF, YOU'RE RIGHT!

The Great Barrier Reef stretches for 1,616 miles off the northeast coast of Australia, and consists of more than 3,000 individual reefs and 900 islands.

(*Wait a minute*, you're thinking. *I thought you said it was alive.*)

It is. Although those islands and undersea reefs look and feel as hard as rock, they're actually made up of millions of tiny animals called coral *polyps*. These little creatures live in vast colonies in the tropical seas of the world. They build hard houses for themselves out of calcium carbonate. As they die, new polyps build new houses on top of the old ones. These polyps are very small, maybe the size of your fingernail, and only grow a few inches per year. But after 10,000 years, that makes for a lot of reef. In fact, it's the Great Barrier Reef—which is almost the same size as California, and the largest structure ever built by living things. (So much for the Empire State Building, the Pyramids, and the Great Wall of China!)

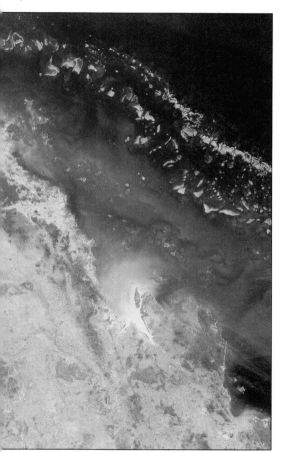

The Great Barrier Reef, seen from space.

It's also one of the richest habitats for marine life in the world. Over 1,500 species of fish call it home. So do 8,000 types of sponges, worms, shellfish, and crustaceans. There are 800 types of starfish and urchins alone. Humpback whales and dolphins breed there. Six of the seven species of sea turtle roam its lagoons. Poisonous sea snakes and jellyfish, too. Dugongs, the gentle cousins of the manatee, loll in its waters. And of course, there are always *lots* of sharks.

SLIMY SEA MOVIES

*These movies will make you want
to stay on land forever.*

1. *The Poseidon Adventure*
(1972)
A cruise ship gets flipped
by a monster wave. Next
time, take a plane to your
vacation spot.

2. *The Abyss* **(1989)**
Aliens with attitude at the
bottom of the ocean. What
could be better?

3. *Titanic* **(1997)**
The biggest ship ever built
runs into an iceberg. Bye-
bye, *Titanic*!

4. *Waterworld* **(1995)**
The polar ice caps have
melted and the entire globe
is covered in water. A peek
at the future after global
warming?

5. *Jaws* **(1975)**
"Just when you thought it
was safe to go back in the
water..." Enough said.

6. *Creature from the Black
Lagoon* **(1954)**
A mutant fish-man terror-
izes the coast of Florida.
Look close, and you can see
the zipper on his costume
when he swims by!

7. *The Incredible Mr.
Limpet* **(1964)**
A nerdy human becomes
a nerdy fish and saves the
world. Yeah, right...

8. *Moby Dick* **(1956)**
Crazy Captain Ahab hunts
the great white whale. Or is
it the other way around?

9. *Deep Rising* **(1998)**
A monster squid attacks a
cruise ship. Help!

10. *The Perfect Storm*
(2000)
An itty-bitty fishing boat
meets a monster wave.
Guess who loses?

KILLER CLAMS...NOT!

A big mollusk with a bad reputation.

Giant clams are big. *Really* big. They can grow to the size of a beach umbrella and weigh over 500 pounds. They're so big that they were once thought to be maneaters—divers told tales of open clams snapping shut on unwary victims and not letting go. Old horror movies were full of scenes of killer clams chomping down scuba divers. The belief was so common that early versions of the U.S. Navy Diving Manual included instructions for escaping a giant clam's death-grip.

Actually, the giant clam is more dangerous out of the water than in: Most giant clam injuries occur when people drop the heavy shells on their toes. In reality, the giant clam closes its shell so slowly that you'd have to be sound asleep not to notice it shutting on you.

The strangest thing about the giant clam is that it's part animal and part plant. Like plants, it uses sunlight to make food. And just like many of the marine animals that share its home on the coral reef, the giant clam filters food from the ocean. With two ways of getting food, maybe that's why they grow so big. One thing's for certain, the giant clam is not a killer—unless of course, someone drops one on your head.

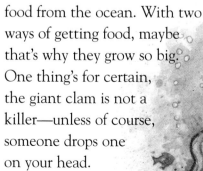

GLOBSTERS

What's shapeless, looks like goop, and really, really stinks?

A *globster* is a very weird, completely baffling object that might be found on any beach. Think of a big pile of jelly-like, fatty flesh. There might be a huge tentacle or a strange-looking

flipper sticking out of the goop. Sometimes it has hair, but it never has bones, scales, or cartilage. And the worst part: It stinks…a lot. Most globsters are eventually identified as the fatty remains of dead whales or giant squids. Some of the hardest to identify have turned out to be dead basking sharks, one of the largest (and strangest) fish in the ocean. But some globsters remain unidentified—a gooey, gross reminder that there are still unsolved mysteries in the deep.

SLIMY SEA FACT

Carolus Linnaeus, the great Swedish scientist who created the naming system we use to label of all living things, was a steadfast believer in sea monsters.

SEA ANIMAL QUIZ #2: BATHING BEAUTY?

1. It's the only marine mammal that can live in fresh or salt water, as long as the water is shallow and warm.

2. Its closest relatives are elephants, hyraxes (a rabbit-sized rodent from the Middle East), and aardvarks.

3. It has three to four fingernails on each of its flippers.

4. It has a mouthful of wide, flat teeth called "marching molars." It constantly replaces them, just like a shark—when one falls out, another moves forward.

5. It has a tail shaped like a paddle.

6. It knows how to have fun in the water. It can do headstands, tail stands, somersaults, barrel rolls—even bodysurf!

7. It farts a lot! That's because it only eats plants—as much as 110 pounds a day.

8. It sounds like a mouse, with squeaks, whistles, and chirps.

9. A grown member of this species can be as big as a pickup truck.

10. When European sailors first saw this creature, they thought it was a mermaid.

WHAT IS IT?

ANSWER:

THE MANATEE

Let's face it—it's hard to imagine how ancient sailors could have mistaken the homely manatee for a beautiful mermaid, but they did. Commonly known as the sea cow, the manatee lives in the warm, shallow coastal waters of Florida, the Caribbean, Central America, Africa, and the Amazon. Its cousin, the *dugong*, lives in the South Pacific and Indian Oceans. Manatees are gentle, slow-moving animals with few natural enemies. In fact, humans are the cause of most manatee deaths. Some get sick from eating old fishing lines. Others get caught in "ghost nets"—nets that break off from fishing boats and drift through the ocean, trapping air-breathing mammals like dolphins, turtles, and manatees under water. But the worst manatee killer is the speedboat: It's a sad fact that researchers use scar patterns from propeller wounds to identify individual manatees.

BEACH TRAFFIC JAM

What do you do when half a million turtles want to lay their eggs at the same time? Get out of the way!

Sea turtles spend most of their lives at sea, traveling thousands of miles as they feed and mate. But every year, the females of all seven sea turtle species—the leatherback, hawksbill, green, loggerhead, Kemp's ridley, olive ridley, and flatback—go back to the beach where they were born to lay their eggs. In Costa Rica this event is called the *arribada*—Spanish for "arrival"—and it's one of the great wonders of nature. During the first or last quarter moon, as many as 5,000 Ridley's turtles swim out of the sea every hour onto a strip of sand less than a mile long. Over the next few nights, 400,000 turtles join them to bury close to 40 million eggs. Why does the *arribada* only happen during a quarter moon? Because that's when the tides, which are controlled by the moon's gravity, are weakest. And that means that the waves will wash away the fewest newly buried eggs. How the turtles figured that out is a mystery.

129

WEIRD SEA FOOD

Uncle John loves sea food—but here are some fish recipes from around the world that might make him want to stick to cheeseburgers.

HÁKARL. If you're ever in Iceland and someone offers you a plate of *hákarl*—run! That's the Icelandic word for "rotten shark," and that's what this dish is. Greenlandic

shark is poisonous when fresh because the meat has lots of uric acid (one of the same acids found in pee). So the clever people of Iceland found a way to make the shark edible. They cut it into big chunks and bury them in a gravel pit for a few months, and when it smells like ammonia instead of pee, they dig it up. Then they hang it up in a shed and let the wind dry it out. When the fish is firm (2–4 months later) it's ready to eat.

Hákarl hanging in a drying shed

FUGU. That's the Japanese name for the poisonous puffer fish or blowfish—and you can die from eating one. The *fugu* is a pretty cool fish. Instead of scales, it has spines like a porcupine. When it's scared, it puffs up and looks like a spiky balloon with fins. (It's also the only fish that can close its eyes.) But the fugu's main claim to fame lies in its guts. They contain *tetrodotoxin*, a poison 1,000 times deadlier than cyanide. In fact, the poison in one fugu can kill 30 people. So naturally, no one would touch this fish with a ten-foot pole, right?

Wrong! Many Japanese consider the fugu the best-tasting fish of all, and aren't afraid to risk their lives to eat it. The Japanese eat 10,000 tons of fugu every year, even though a plate of it can cost $200! Fish restaurants in Japan have "fugu certified" chefs who know how to remove the poisonous parts. Still, even experts make mistakes: Every year, about 100 people die from eating fugu.

SURSTROMMING

What is with the Vikings? First the Icelanders, with their putrefied *hákarl,* and now the Swedes with their favorite disgusting fish dish—*surstromming,* or fermented herring. People have compared its taste to rotten garbage, but it's a traditional treat in Sweden, where they gobble up cans of it by the thousands. It's made by fermenting barrels full of Baltic herring (a small sardine-sized fish) and letting them ferment for months. When the fish are good and stinky, the meat is packed in tin cans and the fermentation goes on. The tin cans often swell up like footballs from all of the gases inside. Airlines in Sweden have banned *surstromming* from their planes because they're afraid a can will explode and shower the passengers with stinky rotten fish. *Bon apetit!*

NINE AMAZING FISH FACTS

These may sound fishy, but Uncle John
swears they are absolutely true.

)● **1. A lobster's teeth are in its stomach.**

)● **2. A shrimp's heart is in its head.**

)● **3. A horseshoe crab has 10 eyes.** They're placed all over its body—even on its tail.

)● **4. You can guess a fish's age by its scales.** You can count the growth rings, just like you'd count the rings on a tree.

)● **5. Fish can get seasick.** Keep a fish in a pail of water on a rolling ship, and sooner or later that fish will barf.

)● **6. Fish get dandruff.** Like humans, it's caused by flaking skin, and there's nothing they can do about it.

)● **7. Some fish can breathe air.** Small fish like *betas* and *gouramis* have an organ called a *labyrinth* that lets them breathe fresh air. It allows them to survive in water with low oxygen levels.

)● **8. Fish can talk to each other.** Some rasp their teeth or make noises in their throats; other fish use their swim bladders like a horn.

)● **9. Fish can change sex.** Boy? Girl? Many fish start out as one sex and turn into the other one later on. Some deepwater fish are both sexes all the time. Then they never need to look for a mate to have babies.

ESCAPE ARTIST

The legendary Houdini claimed he was the greatest
escape artist who ever lived. But he might
have met his match with the octopus.

What has eight arms, two eyes, and a beak? You guessed it. The octopus. It doesn't have a nose, ears, or fingers, but each arm is covered with a double row of white suction cups called  *suckers*. It uses these suckers to explore its world. Each sucker moves by itself like the way we wiggle our toes or fingers. And a sucker not only grips objects, it tastes them. An octopus has a beak like a bird, and a tongue—called a *radula*—that's covered with razor-sharp teeth. These teeth are able to cut through crab and snail shells like a buzzsaw. An octopus will often carry a crab back to its den for dinner. Then, after it's finished eating, the octopus will deposit the shells just outside its den. Very tidy!

The octopus is the great shape-shifter of the sea. It can make itself big and wide like an umbrella, or long and thin like a piece of rope. It can squeeze through cracks under a rock or flatten itself against the walls of a cave. The octopus is also a master of disguise. Its skin can change color instantly, acting as a camouflage to protect it from sharks and other predators.

When it comes to brains, the octopus goes to the head of the class. It is the smartest of all invertebrates. It can find its way through a maze, or figure out how to unscrew the lid of a jar and remove the tasty fish that's inside. The octopus is a very curious creature, and can actually die of boredom if kept in a tank with no world to explore and nothing to entertain it.

It can be pretty sneaky, too. Scientists at an aquarium were baffled by a mysterious disappearing act. Every day they'd place new fish in a tank, but when they returned in the morning, the fish would be gone. Finally they set up a video camera to see who was stealing the fish. They watched in amazement as an octopus in a tank across the room waited for the museum to close, then squeezed its way out of its tank, slid across the floor, slipped into the fish tank, and ate all the fish. Then it crawled back into its own tank and took a nap!

Caught in the act! This octopus is sneaking out its tank through a tiny crack.

SCHOOLBOY SAILOR

Ever dream of going on an adventure? This teen did it.

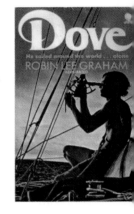

Robin Lee Graham had just turned 16 when he asked his parents for a sailboat. When they asked why, he said, "So I can sail around the world." He didn't even have a driver's license, yet in the summer of 1965 this high school student set sail from Los Angeles on an epic journey. On his tiny 24-foot-long boat, the *Dove*, he took a guitar, a radio, and two kittens for company. He made it to Hawaii...and decided to keep going. Most experienced sailors thought he'd never make it home. Sure, Robin had sailed a lot with his parents during his early teen years. He even knew how to navigate using the stars. But this was a giant trip and he was all alone. Still, Robin kept going.

He survived storms that swept him overboard and broke his mast. He was nearly mowed down by giant tanker ships. Once, he sat dead in the water for 22 days waiting for the wind to blow again. Yet somehow he was able to overcome every obstacle. In the Fiji Islands, he met and married a girl named Patti. But Robin was determined to finish his solo voyage alone. When he finally sailed into the bay of Los Angeles, hundreds of boats came out to greet him. "By the end of my voyage," he said, "I had traveled over 33,000 miles. I was two inches taller and five years older. I was married and soon to be a father. I was a man—but I still couldn't drive a car!"

MERMAIDS

There's something fishy about this tale.

Their Japanese name is *ningyo*. In the Caribbean they're called *aycayia*. West Africans call them *mami wata*. Folk tales of half-human/half-fish creatures go as far back as 1000 BC. And most of these mythical sea folk are female—the *mermaids*.

Mermaids often have long hair, and sing haunting songs that drive sailors mad with longing. Some are said to be able to grant wishes or foretell the future, while others kidnap people and take them to their underwater kingdom. *Selkies* from Scotland, Ireland, and Iceland are rumored to be women who take the shape of seals, then shed their sealskins when they come on land to marry and have children.

But do they really exist? Christopher Columbus thought so. On his journey to the New World, he wrote in his journal that he and his crew spotted mermaids in the Caribbean Sea. He said he was surprised the mermaids were so ugly. (Historians suspect that what Columbus saw were actually manatees, which might resemble humans from a distance because they cradle their young in their arms.)

SPEED SHARK

*Ms. Jaws takes a holiday—and breaks
every speed record known to sharks.*

As great white sharks go, Nicole is not an exceptional specimen. She's only 12 feet long and weighs 3,000 pounds (the biggest great white on record was 23 feet long and weighed 7,000 pounds). But Nicole (named after Australian actress Nicole Kidman) recently did something no other shark has ever done before—she swam farther than any known shark ever swam before, and she did it faster. Nicole swam from South Africa to

Australia and back, a distance of 12,400 miles, and she covered the huge distance in only nine months.

The reason scientists know about Nicole's feat was that she had been tagged with a tracking sensor a few weeks before she embarked on her record-breaking swim. Scientists used to think great whites hung around coastal waters eating the plentiful food that lived there, and didn't venture out into the open ocean. But recent research seems to indicate otherwise. Scientists were hoping that Nicole's sensor would provide them with some clues as to where the sharks went, and why.

Their best guess is that Nicole was husband-hunting, since she had lots of food in South Africa year round and had no reason to look for it elsewhere. But what surprised the scientists was how Nicole swam straight as an arrow across the ocean. Although she dove frequently, sometimes as deep as 3,000 feet, Nicole spent more than half her swim time right at the surface. Shark researcher Ramon Bonfil thinks Nicole was using the stars and moon to find her way to Australia, and back again.

So, did Nicole find a boyfriend on her trip to Australia? If she did, she's not telling.

DID YOU KNOW?
Even though it looks like a jellyfish, the *blue bottle jellyfish*, better known as the *Portuguese Man of War*, is actually a colony of 4 different tiny animals called *zooids*. Some of the zooids make the bell, others the stinging tentacles, another the stomach. All of them work together to make one nasty sea beastie! Swimmers around the world know to avoid the beach when an armada of blue bottles drift in.

SURFIN' SNAILS

They ride the surf to catch their dinner!

The *plough snail* from South Africa likes to eat dead things that have been washed up onto the beach. When this super-sensitive snail detects the chemical traces of something good and dead in the water, it makes a beeline for the carcass—but not by leaving a slime trail across the sand like any other snail. No, this snail surfs! It uses its large fleshy foot like a surfboard to ride the waves right to its food. Its unique way of getting up and down the beach makes the plough snail the fastest snail in the world.

THE SLIMY "SEE"

Brian Reel and the folks at Aqua One Technologies were sitting on this idea for a long time. Now you can sit on it, too. It's the Fish n' Flush, the only toilet in the world with a built-in aquarium.

Brian adds that if you don't like fish, you can make it into a terrarium and put other animals in there—like lizards, snakes, and scorpions.

PHOTO CREDITS